First World War
and Army of Occupation
War Diary
France, Belgium and Germany

41 DIVISION
Divisional Troops
Royal Army Service Corps
Divisional Train (296, 297, 298, 299 Companies ASC)
28 April 1916 - 31 October 1919

WO95/2631/1

The Naval & Military Press Ltd
www.nmarchive.com
Published in association with The National Archives

Published by

The Naval & Military Press Ltd

Unit 10 Ridgewood Industrial Park,

Uckfield, East Sussex,

TN22 5QE England

Tel: +44 (0) 1825 749494

www.naval-military-press.com

www.nmarchive.com

This diary has been reprinted in facsimile from the original. Any imperfections are inevitably reproduced and the quality may fall short of modern type and cartographic standards.

© **Crown Copyright**
Images reproduced by permission of The National Archives, London, England, 2015.

Contents

Document type	Place/Title	Date From	Date To
Heading	WO95/2631/1 41 Div. Train		
Heading	BEF H.Q. 41 Div Train 1916 Apl-1917 Oct. 1918 Mar-1919 Oct. In Italy 1917 Nov-1918 Feb.		
War Diary	Strazeele	28/04/1916	31/05/1916
War Diary	La Creche	01/06/1916	31/07/1916
Heading	War Diary Of 41st Divisional Train. A.S.C. from 1st August 16 to 31st August 16 Volume 4.		
War Diary	La Creche	01/08/1916	17/08/1916
War Diary	Fletre	18/08/1916	24/08/1916
War Diary	Long	25/08/1916	05/09/1916
War Diary	Argoeuves	06/09/1916	06/09/1916
War Diary	Buire	07/09/1916	11/09/1916
War Diary	Albert	12/09/1916	18/09/1916
War Diary	Buire	19/09/1916	02/10/1916
War Diary	Becordel	03/10/1916	04/10/1916
War Diary	Quarry	05/10/1916	06/10/1916
War Diary	Quarry (E.11.c)	07/10/1916	11/10/1916
War Diary	Buire	12/10/1916	16/10/1916
War Diary	Argoeuves	17/10/1916	17/10/1916
War Diary	Hallancourt	18/10/1916	19/10/1916
War Diary	Fletre	20/10/1916	24/10/1916
War Diary	Reninghelst	25/10/1916	31/10/1916
War Diary	Reninghelst. Sheet 28 G.34.d Central.	01/11/1916	26/06/1917
War Diary	Reninghelst Sheet 28 M.4 Central	27/06/1917	30/06/1917
War Diary	Meteren Sheet 27 X.15.d.7.5	01/07/1917	23/07/1917
War Diary	Boeschepe Sheet 27 R.9.d.9.4	24/07/1917	25/07/1917
War Diary	Westoutre Sheet 28 M.15.a.6.8.	26/07/1917	15/08/1917
War Diary	Meteren Sheet 27 X.15.d.7.5	16/08/1917	21/08/1917
War Diary	Wizernes Sheet 36d. N.E. F.2.d.8.2	22/08/1917	15/09/1917
War Diary	Zevecoten Sheet 28 N.W. G.35.c.3.5	16/09/1917	23/09/1917
War Diary	Caestre Sheet 27. S.E W.3.a.4.5.	24/09/1917	27/09/1917
War Diary	La Panne Sheet 11. W.15.a.5.2.	28/09/1917	07/10/1917
War Diary	St. Idesbalde Sheet 11. W.10.b.1.6.	08/10/1917	29/10/1917
War Diary	Rosendael	30/10/1917	31/10/1917
War Diary	Camposampiero Italy	01/03/1918	05/03/1918
War Diary	Lucheux France	06/03/1918	20/03/1918
War Diary	France	21/03/1918	31/03/1918
War Diary	Authie France	01/04/1918	01/04/1918
War Diary	Halloy	02/04/1918	02/04/1918
War Diary	Steenvoorde	03/04/1918	10/04/1918
War Diary	G.4.a.3.0. Sheet 28.	11/04/1918	12/04/1918
War Diary	G.4.a.3.0.	13/04/1918	26/04/1918
War Diary	Sheet 28. A.16.a.8.4	27/04/1918	30/04/1918
War Diary	Sheet 27 F.21.d.1.2	01/05/1918	15/05/1918
War Diary	Sheet 27 F.16.d.9.0	16/05/1918	04/06/1918
War Diary	Nieurlet France	05/06/1918	07/06/1918
War Diary	Eperlecques France	08/06/1918	26/06/1918
War Diary	Oudezeele France	27/06/1918	02/07/1918
War Diary	K.21.b.8.5 Sheet 27.	03/07/1918	29/08/1918
War Diary	Wizernes France	30/08/1918	02/09/1918

War Diary	K.24.a.9.8. Sheet 27.	03/09/1918	27/09/1918
War Diary	Dallington Camp Sheet 27 L.29.c.8.2.	28/09/1918	28/09/1918
War Diary	Dominion Camp Sheet 28. G.23.b.8.4	29/09/1918	04/10/1918
War Diary	Lankhof Camp Sheet 28. I.26.c.0.1	05/10/1918	16/10/1918
War Diary	Dadizeele Sheet 28 K.12.c.2.1	17/10/1918	21/10/1918
War Diary	Bisseghem Sheet 29. G.36.a.2.7.	22/10/1918	29/10/1918
War Diary	Courtrai Sheet 29/ N.2.b.3.8.	30/10/1918	02/11/1918
War Diary	Sweveghem Sheet 29/ O.1.a.6.5	03/11/1918	05/11/1918
War Diary	Esscher Sheet 29/I.32.b.1.1	06/11/1918	07/11/1918
War Diary	Snephoek Sheet 29/I.9.b.7.2	08/11/1918	09/11/1918
War Diary	Ingoyhem Sheet 29/J.27.d.9.1	10/11/1918	11/11/1918
War Diary	Kerkhem Sheet 30 M.14.d.9.1	12/11/1918	15/11/1918
War Diary	Nederbrakel Sheet 30 N.17.	16/11/1918	18/11/1918
War Diary	Santbergen Sheet 30/Q.15	19/11/1918	21/11/1918
War Diary	Grammont Sheet 30. V.2.	22/11/1918	12/12/1918
War Diary	Enghien	13/12/1918	13/12/1918
War Diary	Hal	14/12/1918	14/12/1918
War Diary	Brain L'Alleud	15/12/1918	17/12/1918
War Diary	Marbais	18/12/1918	18/12/1918
War Diary	Mazy	19/12/1918	19/12/1918
War Diary	Waret Le Chaussee	20/12/1918	20/12/1918
War Diary	Huy	21/12/1918	09/01/1919
War Diary	Huy	05/01/1919	11/01/1919
War Diary	Cologne Germany	12/01/1919	30/04/1919
War Diary	Marienburg Coln Germany	01/05/1919	31/07/1919
War Diary	Coln Germany	01/08/1919	31/08/1919
War Diary	Marienburg Cologne	01/09/1919	31/10/1919
Miscellaneous	41st. Divisional Train A.S.C. Statement of Casualties from May 1916 to 30th. Septr. 1917.	30/09/1917	30/09/1917
Heading	Historical Record of 41st Divisional Train. 296:297:298:299 (H.T.) Coys. Army Service.		
Heading	Historical Record of No. 41 Divisional Train 296, 297, 298, Coys. (H.T.) A.S.C.		
Miscellaneous	Historical Record of No. 41 Divisional Train.		
Miscellaneous	Appendix "A". Commanding Officers.		
Miscellaneous	Appendix "B" Honours and Awards.		
Miscellaneous	Appendix "C" Casualties Amongst Personnel.		
Miscellaneous	Appendix "D" Casualties to Horses and Vehicles.		
Miscellaneous	Appendix "E" Company Moves.		
Miscellaneous	Appendix "F" Prizes Won at Horse Shows.		

WO95/2631/1
41 Div. Train

BEF

HQ. 41 Div
TRAIN
1916 APL — 1917 OCT
1918 MAR — 1919 OCT
In ITALY 1917 NOV — 1918 FEB

Army Form C. 2118

41 Div Train

WAR DIARY or INTELLIGENCE SUMMARY
(Erase heading not required.)

Vol 1

Place	Date	Hour	Summary of Events and Information	Remarks and references to Appendices
STRAZEELE	28/4/16 to 3-5-16		S.S.O. and Supply Officers arrive. Billets arranged. Report at II"d Army for 2nd for instructions. Details fed by Corps Troops Supply Officer 5th Corps. Supply duties for division arranged	
"	4.5.16		TRAIN HQ. 2rs detrain at STEENBECQUE also H.d 2r. Coy. no casualties, all proceed by march route to STRAZEELE and go into Billets. weather fine.	
"	5.5.16		Refilling from Railhead (HAZEBROUCK GARBE) by Horse Transport commenced. No.2 Coy. TRAIN detrain at SODEWAERSVELDE, Capt. Kemp left at HAVRE sick no other casualties. Go into Billets at OUTTERSTEIN	
"	6.5.16		Refilling with Column commenced. Refilling Point arranged, satisfactory progress. No.3 Coy. TRAIN detrain at SODEWAERSVELDE no casualties. weather fine. go into Billets at STRAZEELE.	
"	7.5.16		No.4 Coy. TRAIN detrain at STEENBECQUE no casualties. Go into Billets at WALLON CAPPEL	
"	8.5.16		TRAIN now working as organization. C.O. visits all Billets. Baggage and Supply Vehicles withdrawn from units and held with Train Companies weather wet.	
"	9.5.16		No. 2 Coy. move into BAILLEUL Area with 122nd Infantry Brigade. " 3 Coy. move into OUTTERSTEIN Area with 124th Infantry Brigade	
"	10.5.16		Railhead changed to STEENWERCK. Supplies for 124th Brigade field into H.T. Wagons from railhead direct. Some rain	
"	11.5.16		Two Daimler Cars taken from formation and sent to ARMY Troops Supply Coln. II'd Army	

WAR DIARY
or
INTELLIGENCE SUMMARY
(Erase heading not required.)

Army Form C. 2118

Instructions regarding War Diaries and Intelligence Summaries are contained in F.S. Regs., Part II. and the Staff Manual respectively. Title Pages will be prepared in manuscript.

Place	Date	Hour	Summary of Events and Information	Remarks and references to Appendices
STRAZEELE	12.5.16		Operation order No 15 received (Apdx I) Lce H.P. Horne died "Pneumonia"	
"	13.5.16		Orders to move held in abeyance weather fine	
"	14.5.16		Brass received cavalry orders no 15. Two horses evacuated to Vet. Hospital	
"	15.5.16		Weather very fine. No change in procedure.	
"	16.5.16		— do — — do —	
"	17.5.16		Routine work. Weather fine.	
"	18.5.16		Two men join from 15th Hants Regt. for Bataan tuition to rec. offs	
"	19.5.16		Information received re Cristo Beans in extraction taken, details from 138th Field Amb.	
"	20.5.16		On reorganization join train details from P.S.G. 140th Field Amb. Information from 12th casualty clearing station. Death of IP026803 Pte FAWCETT, M.T. 2DCoy on 18 inst. Pneumonia. Reorganization scheme for Company + train repairs to D.H.Qrs All kits of formation inspected	
"	21.5.16		Routine work, weather fine exercise bath.	
"	22.5.16		Pte Shotin tried by F.G.C.M. sentenced to 42 days 2 P No 2 spoknote	
"	23.5.16		Routine Work	
"	24.5.16		7 draughts horses to Remounts on reorganization of A.S.C. 3 sergeants and 6 drivers to Base Inspection of Augmentals transport of 138th, 139th, 140th Field Ambulances. Alteration of Refilling Point.	
"	25.5.16			
"	26.5.16		Head 2D. Company move to La CRECHE	

WAR DIARY
or
INTELLIGENCE SUMMARY
(Erase heading not required.)

Army Form C. 2118

Place	Date	Hour	Summary of Events and Information	Remarks and references to Appendices
STRAZEELE	27.5.16		Drivers Jeans & Johnson tried by F.G.C.M. sentenced to 61 days F.P.№1	
"	28.5.16		Captain Kemp rejoins from hospital. Routine work	
"	29.5.16		Routine work	
"	30.5.16		Some Rain. Head Qrs. Train move to La CRECHE	
"	31.5.16		Nos. 2 and 4 Companies move to La CRECHE	

W. W. Thodory. Lt. Col.
COMMDG. 41st DIVNL. TRAIN, A.S.C.

Army Form C. 2118

WAR DIARY
or
INTELLIGENCE SUMMARY
(Erase heading not required.)

Instructions regarding War Diaries and Intelligence Summaries are contained in F.S. Regs., Part II. and the Staff Manual respectively. Title Pages will be prepared in manuscript.

Place	Date	Hour	Summary of Events and Information	Remarks and references to Appendices
LA CRECHE	1-6-15		All Companies & Train now concentrated in this area. Tieing at Railhead & supplies now taken over by Train (Horse transport)	[sig]
—"—	2.6.15		Some rain, routine procedure	[sig]
—"—	3.6.15		Routine procedure. Two men admitted to Hospital	[sig]
—"—	4.6.15		Routine procedure. Some rain	[sig]
—"—	5.6.15		Inspection of all 1st Line Transport & 122nd Inf/y Bde by D.C. Train	[sig]
—"—	6.6.15		Showery all day;	[sig]
—"—	7.6.15		1 Sergt. 10 drivers 10 wagons with horses moved to ARMENTIERES for duty with R.E. to be attached to R.E.'s	[sig]
—"—	8.6.15		Routine procedure, 2 cases of Sick discovered in Coys. Pte Andrew to H. 2/L. Holland returns from Hospital	[sig]
—"—	9.6.15		Routine procedure.	[sig]
—"—	10.6.15		One french interpreter leaves for transfer to another formation	[sig]
—"—	11.6.15		Routine procedure, several cases of Sick discovered and sent to Field Amb.	[sig]
—"—	12.6.15		Much rain, inspection by D.C. Train & 2 Battalions 122nd Inf/y Bde, 1st Line transport. M.O. has a sparine inspection of all ranks & cases of Sick discovered. Lt Andrew rejoins from H.	[sig]
—"—	13.6.15		One H.D. Horse received from Remount dept:	[sig]
—"—	14.6.15		No change. Time advanced one hour at 11pm (becomes midnight)	[sig]

WAR DIARY
or
INTELLIGENCE SUMMARY
(Erase heading not required.)

Army Form C. 2118

Instructions regarding War Diaries and Intelligence Summaries are contained in F.S. Regs., Part II. and the Staff Manual respectively. Title Pages will be prepared in manuscript.

Place	Date	Hour	Summary of Events and Information	Remarks and references to Appendices
Pt Creche	15.6.16		No change	2/Lt Pullen to Pt.
-"-	16.6.16		3 Men evacuated to Hospital. Horse inspection. Gas attack about Runcuyht - no casualties	App
-"-	17.6.16		No change	App
-"-	18.6.16		Inspection of 1st Line Transport 123rd J.B.	App
-"-	19.6.16		No change. Inspection of 1st Line Transport 124th Infantry Brigade, also inspection of 3rd & 4th Coy Train	App
-"-	20.6.16		Inspection of remainder 1st Line Transport 124th Infy Bd. also 2 Coy Train 2 R.Y and 4 H.D. teams B 123-124 machine Gun Companies	App
-"-	21.6.16		C.O. visits Army Head Quarters. Maples & 3 Coy Train	App
-"-	22.6.16		Routine procedure. 1 G.S. Wagon (surplus) handed over to 20th D.A.C.	App
-"-	23.6.16		Routine procedure	App
-"-	24.6.16		Routine procedure. Reinforcements join. 2/Lt Pullene ASC. rejoins from Hospital	App
-"-	25.6.16			
-"-	26.6.16		Routine procedure, much rain	App
-"-	27.6.16			
-"-	28.6.16		No change	App
-"-	29.6.16		Trouble re-fill for 30th inst. 1st proc. Previous ration for latter date	App
-"-	30.6.16		Supplies from Railhead drawn as usual and taken to supply column there to be dumped	App

W.W. Moloney, Col
COMMD'G. 41st DIVNL. TRAIN, A.S.C.

July

41 Army Form C.2118

41st DIVL. TRAIN, A.S.C. 41 Div Train

WAR DIARY
or
INTELLIGENCE SUMMARY
(Erase heading not required.)

Vol 3

Instructions regarding War Diaries and Intelligence Summaries are contained in F.S. Regs., Part II. and the Staff Manual respectively. Title Pages will be prepared in manuscript.

Place	Date	Hour	Summary of Events and Information	Remarks and references to Appendices
LA CRECHE	1-7-16		Capt. Priestlim joins from 39th Train for duty as S.S.O.	
–"–	2.7.16		Major Traice leaves to join 3 Divisional Train to take over Command	
–"–	3.7.16		Convoy out at 10-30pm in connection with Gas Duties returned 6-30am 4th	
–"–	4-7-16		S.O.S. visits train and makes casual inspection. 2 horses to mobile vet team	
–"–	5.7.16		Enquiry made by 2/S.C. Maxted for discharging a loaded convoy and sentenced to 3 months F.P. No 1. Convoy out at 10-30pm in connection with Gas Duties returns 6am 6th	
–"–	6.7.16		6 R.& reinforcements arrive; 2 brums to Hospital.	
–"–	7-7-16		Captain Robertson ASC to Hospital.	
–"–	8-7-16		Routine procedure	
–"–	9-7-16		Inspection of all Horses on parade by C.O.	
–"–	10-7-16		One man to 2nd Army Head Quarters for duty as Servant. One horse evacuated to Wty team. Convoy of 15 Wagons to SODEWAERSWELDE to Special Brigade R.E. for accessories	
–"–	11-7-16		Convoy of 20 Wagons to Special Brigade R.E. STEENWERCK for accessories. Conveying to Trench.	
–"–	12.7.16		Routine procedure. O'Smick to Base Hospital	
–"–	13.7.16		Routine procedure	
–"–	14.7.16		Routine procedure. One G.S. Limbered Wagon 1082 1/L2 H.T. Stores to ABBEVILLE (surplus)	
–"–	15-7-16		Inspection of Horses lung, Lungs & all Companies	
–"–	16.7.16			
–"–	17-7-16		Convoy for Gas accessories 8 16 Wagons 10pm to 6am	

Army Form C. 2118

WAR DIARY
or
INTELLIGENCE SUMMARY
(Erase heading not required.)

Instructions regarding War Diaries and Intelligence Summaries are contained in F.S. Regs., Part II. and the Staff Manual respectively. Title Pages will be prepared in manuscript.

Place	Date	Hour	Summary of Events and Information	Remarks and references to Appendices
La Creche	18.7.16		3 Lorries & 4 L. Wagons & Horses taken from 122, 123, 124 Bn M.G.S. (Surplus) S.N.C. O⁴ and men Infantry train for duty in Divisional Boot repairing Staff. OC attends conference 11 days	
-do-	19.7.16		Pte Seagrove leaves for Etaples. BETHUNE on posting (5 R.T.C. 1 R.A.) Horse from IX Palmer Bolton 1 H.D. Hessex to Remounts. Convoy of 33 Wagons for Sus accessories	
-do-	20.7.16		Convoy to Hospital. Captain Haynard C.? Pois for attachment Pte. T.A.G. P Gale H.J.L Janis from posted to H.Q Coy	
-do-	21.7.16		1 Wagon to 171 Tunnelling Coy R.E. Baggage. Supply Wagons "A" Echelon & X C to join them 1 man to H. Base 2 H.D. Horses to Remounts	
-do-	22.7.16		Inspection of W. D. 122 Bn M.G. Coy by S2	
-do-	23.7.16		-do- 123 -"-	
-do-	24.7.16		Capt. Fleming to Command 3 Coy. Capt. Laid to I.O. 4 Coy. 2/Lt Rooke to 4 Coy for Transport Lt Neville to I.O. 3 Coy. 2/Lt Holland to 1 Coy. Transport Inspection of 124 B. M. G. Coy by Co. 1 Lorry, 17 Wagons for Sus accessories	
-do-	25.7.16		1 Bs. Wagon Transferred to H.A.G. Anzac to Convoy, 17 kegs for Sus accessory	
-do-	26.7.16		W.O & P Barter (deserter from this formation) found to be serving under 41 Sypal Coy	
-do-	27.7.16		Inspection of W. O⁴. 1 & 2 Coys Tram dismantled awaiting orders 1 m. T. Coy Janus from 2nd Army troops Supply Col for attachment	

WAR DIARY
or
INTELLIGENCE SUMMARY
(Erase heading not required.)

Army Form C. 2118

Place	Date	Hour	Summary of Events and Information	Remarks and references to Appendices
LA CRECHE	28/7/16		Inspection of No. 3 & 4 Coys Tream transport marching order. 1 man admitted to F.A. and struck off strength	[sig]
"	29/7/16		Routine duty and transport work. Inspection of Water Carts 122nd S.B.	[sig]
"	30/7/16		Two horses destroyed by ghee fire also 1 G.S. wagon at ARMENTIERES (H.Q. 2nd Coy) I Pt. Thift R.S.C. joined and is posted to 2 Coy Train	[sig]
"	30/7/16		Inspection of Water Carts 123rd S.B.	[sig]

W. W. Thoburn Lt Col.

Confidential.

War Diary
of
41st Divisional Train. A.S.C.
from 1st August /16 to 31st August /16.
Volume 4

V.W. Molony Lieut-Colonel
Comdg 41st Divl Train.

WAR DIARY or INTELLIGENCE SUMMARY

Army Form C. 2118

Place	Date	Hour	Summary of Events and Information	Remarks and references to Appendices
LA CRECHE	1.8.16		Informal inspection by O.C. Weather hot.	
"	2.8.16		Capt. W.H. SHEFFIELD R.A.M.C. from Div. train to RFA as M.O. a/c Capt. E.S. MOORHEAD R.A.M.C. from RFA to Div. train as M.O. a/c Weather hot	
"	3.8.16		2 Lieut H.L. HOLLARD admitted to 138 F.A. 2 Lt G.C. HOLMAN posted to R.F.C. No T4/108222 L/ HATCH J.W. struck off the strength.	
		4 pm	M/c chair visits H. Qrs & looks for baggage. Baggage & supply wagons temporary attached again 20th M.T.s & derby Regt. Weather hot.	
"	4.8.16		Lorry & crew attached for supplies to 20th M.T.s & derby Regt. approx 2 m A.T. supply above D.S. Weather hot.	
"	5.8.16		3 Horses struck off strength. No T4/099240 Dr CARLING H. struck off the strength. D.D.R. injuries. 24 H.D. horses being exchanged for 24 L.D. horses an escort of Dr. Lam. 5 Lorry and crew taken in strength temporary attached for supplies 24 H.D. returned to Remounts.	
		4/pm	24 L.D. returned from Remounts. Gas alert returned Weather hot.	
"	6.8.16		Evacuation to Base from 12 C.C.S. of 2 Lieut H.L. HOLLARD Evacuation to Base (of No.T4/093264 S/ATTEWELL A.J. M.4 coy) [instructed to Depot] (received on 5.8.16). Weather hot	
"	7.8.16		8 men reinforcements join from Base (6.8.16) Taken on Strength & posted:— 5 H. Qr. Coy & 3 to No 3 Coy. 1 HD Horse struck off the strength. Weather cold.	
"	8.8.16	9 am	D.O. visits Sir. A. Qrs. 1 HD Horse died and struck off strength Weather hot.	

WAR DIARY or INTELLIGENCE SUMMARY

Army Form C. 2118

Place	Date	Hour	Summary of Events and Information	Remarks and references to Appendices
LA CRECHE	9.8.16	10 a.m.	C.O. attends G.C.M. at BAILLEUL	& "
		11 a.m.	Inspection of Water Carts of 124 Inf. Bde. Party dismissed. Weather hot.	
"	10.8.16	4.45 a.m.	10 Wagons on transport duty for R.E. 10 Wagons on transport duty for R.E. (at 8 a.m.) Inspection of water carts of 124 Inf. Bde. completed. 1 H.D. Horse No 4 boy destroyed. Weather hot.	& "
"	11.8.16	8 a.m.	Company conduct sheets checked with M.C. boys	& "
		8 a.m.	20 Wagons on transport duty for R.E. No T2/11143 & CHARLES. T. No 4 boy struck off strength. Weather hot.	& "
"	12.8.16		1 Riding horse cast by D.D.R. + transferred to No 52 Mobile Vet. Section. Weather hot.	& "
"	13.8.16		Routine and supplies as usual. Weather hot.	& "
"	14.8.16		Baggage wagons for units of 12 2 Bde. from at 6 p.m. A.S.C. detachments attached R.E. upon 14 gun boy. Rebuilding commenced at 9.45 a.m. (Sunday only) Informal inspection at refilling. Present Weather hot.	& "
"	15.8.16		Baggage wagons for units of 123 Bde. from 6 p.m. Baggage wagons for units 19th Middlesex from 6 p.m. Weather hot.	& "
"	16.8.16		Baggage wagons for units of 124 Bde. from 6 p.m. Wagon for extra storage returns to C.R.E. for Sanitary duty 2 M.Q. train moved from LA CRECHE to CAESTRE 11 Mules + 2 Riders received from Remounts. Weather hot.	& "
"	17.8.16		Train H.Qrs. moved from LA CRECHE to FLETRE + No 3 boy train from LA CRECHE to METEREN. Weather showery.	& "

WAR DIARY
or
INTELLIGENCE SUMMARY
(Erase heading not required.)

Army Form C. 2118

Place	Date	Hour	Summary of Events and Information	Remarks and references to Appendices
FLETRE	18/8/16		No 4 Coy from LA CRECHE to NOTRE BOOM. 11 Mules & 2 Riders received from Field Remount Station. Weather hot	
"	19/8/16		Routine & Supplies as usual	
"	20/8/16		H. Qrs. Coy from LA CRECHE to FLETRE	
"	21/8/16		No 14/1929 H Pte DUNFORD R.E. joined from Base and posted to No 3 Coy. 1 Rider + 5 H.D. Horses taken on the strength and posted as follows:- 1 Rider + 1 H.D. to H.Q. Coy. 1 H.D. to No 2 Coy. 2 H.D. to No 3 Coy. 1 H.D. to No 4 Coy. Weather hot	
"	22/8/16		1 H.D. Horse No 2 Coy struck off the strength. Weather showery	
"	23/8/16	3.25am	No 4 Coy from NOTRE BOOM to LONG entrain at BAILLEUL. W detrain at PONT REMY	
		11 am	No 3 Coy from METEREN to LONG entrain at BAILLEUL MAIN detrain at LONGPRE. Weather showery	
"	24/8/16	6 am	H.Q. Train + B.Q. Coy from FLETRE to LONG entrain at BAILLEUL W detrain at PONT REMY	
		2 pm	No 2 Coy from CAESTRE to LONG entrain at BAILLEUL (MAIN) & detrain at LONGPRE. No 14/09 4152 Pte FEAR IS. N. Qrs Coy injured severely alleged to have been kicked from truck by a mule and a train passing in the opposite direction passed over his leg and the thing foot. Transferred to No 13 General Hospital. Weather fog and the thing foot	
LONG	25/8/16		1 Rider struck off the strength. Weather showery	
"	26/8/16		No 1/3556 1 St Duck K.E.G. No 4 Coy transferred to Reinforcement B.H.T.D. Havre. G.O. + adjusted visit H. Army St. Qrd. Weather showery	

Army Form C. 2118

WAR DIARY
or
INTELLIGENCE SUMMARY
(Erase heading not required.)

Instructions regarding War Diaries and Intelligence Summaries are contained in F.S. Regs., Part II. and the Staff Manual respectively. Title Pages will be prepared in manuscript.

Place	Date	Hour	Summary of Events and Information	Remarks and references to Appendices
LONG	27.8.16		1 Riding Horse transferred from A. Qno. boy. to No 3 boy. Weather showery	
"	28.8.16		Routine & supplies as usual. Weather showery	
"	29.8.16		Routine work as usual. Weather very wet	
"	30.8.16		Routine work as usual. Weather very wet	
"	31.8.16	10.30am	Lt. J. WHYTE tried by F.C.M. Two orders taken on the strength and posted to A. Qno boy. Weather fine	

J.B. ——— Capt.
D. COMMDG. 61st DIVL. TRAIN, A.S.C.

WAR DIARY or INTELLIGENCE SUMMARY

Army Form C. 2118

Hdl Divl Train A.S.C.

Place	Date	Hour	Summary of Events and Information	Remarks and references to Appendices
LONG	1/9/16	10.45	H.Q. included 1st Line Transport of 124th Infantry Brigade.	
		11.30	" " " " 125th " "	
			No. 040680145. Dr MURFITT W. evacuated to the NEW ZEALAND STATIONARY H AMIENS on 27/8/16, are struck	R.2
			No. 040413500. Dr WADE W. off the strength of this formation	
			No. 050627720. Dr ALDRIDGE H.T. evacuated to the NEW ZEALAND STATIONARY H AMIENS, on 30/8/16, to struck off strength.	
			No. 036555 Dr FORD C. } " " " " " on 31/8/16, are " " "	
			No. 036312 Dr PASSMORE G. }	
			1 H.D. HORSE destroyed — struck off strength.	
		17.0.	H.Q. included No. 3-4 Coys full marching order parade	
		14.50	HQrs Coy move off. Proceeding from LONG to ARGOEUVES, to be under orders of C.R.A. H.Q. Divn	
			Weather DULL	
"	2/9/16	10.15	6.0 included 1st Line Transport of 132nd Infantry Brigade.	R.2
			Weather FINE	
			Routine Work.	
"	3/9/16		Divl. Horse Show. 10.10 "A.M." Malgring	R.7
			No. 036555. Dr FORD C. reports from H.P. & is taken on strength & posted to No 4 Coy	
			3 H.D. HORSES evacuated from MOBILE VETERINARY SECTION. & are struck off Strength.	
			Weather:— A thunder storm in the evening. Otherwise FINE	
"	4/9/16		1 Mule. No. 3 Coy destroyed — struck off strength.	R.7
			Weather. FINE. MUCH SUNSHINE	
			General Routine Work. No. T/1/OH/52. A/CSM. MATTHEWS. C.E. No 3 Coy proceed for duty with 138 Field Ambulance.	
"	5/9/16		Train H. Qrs. No 2, & 3 Coys move from LONG to ARGOEUVES. T/CAPT. C.M.B. SIMES. A.V.C.	R.7
			CO commands the Road Transport for the Division during the move. posted to Command. M.V.S.	
			Weather DAMP. T/CAPT. F.V. PERRY A.V.C. from	
			No. 031026053. A/S.Sjt. MACKENZIE E. 138 Field Ambulance rejoins Train & is posted to No 3 Coy	

Army Form C. 2118

WAR DIARY
or
INTELLIGENCE SUMMARY
(Erase heading not required.)

Instructions regarding War Diaries and Intelligence Summaries are contained in F.S. Regs., Part II. and the Staff Manual respectively. Title Pages will be prepared in manuscript.

Place	Date	Hour	Summary of Events and Information	Remarks and references to Appendices
ARGOEUVES	6/9/16		H.Qrs Train, No. 2, & 3 Coys arrive at camp at BUIRE. No 4 Coy move from LONG to CAMP at BUIRE. Weather FAIR.	L.J.
BUIRE.	7/9/16		No 4 Coy arrive BUIRE. Weather FINE.	L.J.
"	8/9/16		2/Lieut. H.L. HOLLARD taken on strength as per orders received from BASE that no officers must be struck off without their authority. 1 Mule received from Remounts posted to No 3 Coy. Weather FINE.	L.J.
"	9/9/16		Court of Enquiry assembles to enquire into injuries received by No. 17/36513. Dr PASSMORE.G. evacuated from No 3 Coy. PRESIDENT T/CAPT. B.W. PARKER MEMBERS {LT. C. TRIPP, T/2nd LT. C.F. LOCHNER Weather FAIR.	L.J.
"	10/9/16		Court as per 9/9/16 reassembles to enquire into injuries received by No. T4/091152. Dr FEARS. M. H.Qrs Coy. No T2/SR/02119. Dr SMITH. J.S. No 1 Coy evacuated to the NEW ZEALAND STATIONARY H.P. AMIENS. & struck off strength. 2. H.D. HORSES rec'd from Remounts posted to No 3 Coy. 1 H.D. HORSE H.Qrs Coy struck off evacuated to MOBILE VETERINARY SECTION. Weather FINE.	L.J.

WAR DIARY
or
INTELLIGENCE SUMMARY
(Erase heading not required.)

Army Form C. 2118

Instructions regarding War Diaries and Intelligence Summaries are contained in F. S. Regs., Part II. and the Staff Manual respectively. Title Pages will be prepared in manuscript.

Place	Date	Hour	Summary of Events and Information	Remarks and references to Appendices
BUIRE	10/9/16		Advd train move from camp at BUIRE to ALBERT. Weather FINE.	R.T.
ALBERT	12/9/16		1 H.D. HORSE. No 2 Coy evacuated to M.V. Secn - struck off strength. Weather SHOWERY.	R.T.
	13/9/16	23.0	Routine work. H Coy officer attend train HQrs offrs re "Search Operation Orders" Reed. Weather MUCH RAIN.	R.T.
	14/9/16		Baggage wagons from units. 2 H.D. HORSES evacuated from H.QRS Coy to M.V.S. - from thence to CLEARING Ft. struck off strength. 2 H.D HORSES recd from Remounts, posted to HQrs Coy. Weather FINE	R.T.
	15/9/16		Train awaiting orders to move, packed up in case of any great emergency. Weather FINE	R.T.
	16/9/16		Do at 15/9/16. SHELLS drop in the vicinity of HQrs train. Weather FINE	R.T.
	17/9/16		Do at 15/9/16. Shells drop in the vicinity of HQrs train. HQrs train Horse lines moved during shelling. Weather FINE	R.T.
	18/9/16		HQrs 2, 3 & 4 Coys move from ALBERT to old camping ground at BUIRE. Weather HEAVY RAIN.	R.T.

Army Form C. 2118

WAR DIARY
or
INTELLIGENCE SUMMARY
(Erase heading not required.)

Instructions regarding War Diaries and Intelligence Summaries are contained in F.S. Regs., Part II and the Staff Manual respectively. Title Pages will be prepared in manuscript.

Place	Date	Hour	Summary of Events and Information	Remarks and references to Appendices
BUIRE	19/9/16		4 O.R. Coy move from ALBERT to BUIRE. 1 Tpgl. & 1 H.D. Horse evacuated from M.V. Secn. – struck off Strength. 2 funds: As Surplus to Establishment returned to Havre, on authority of D.A.G. Base. Weather. MUCH RAIN	L. 1
	20/9/16		Routine Work. Weather. RAIN to FINE	L. 1
	21/9/16		No TO/10113. Dr. SEARS, E. No & Coy evacuated to No. 38 CASUALTY CLEARING STATION, & struck off 1 H.D. Horse, H.Q. Coy wounded in stomach & foot by Shrapnel. Gravely destroyed. struck off Weather. FINE.	L. 1
	22/9/16		No. 31419. L/Cpl. QUIBBLE, H. reporno 124 M.G. Coy having passed a satisfactory course of instruction in held shooting. 2 H.D. HORSES. H.Qrs. Coy evacuated from M.V.Secn. struck off strength. 10-16.30 Horses farms terminating cleaned up for inspection by C.O. at 4 - 4.30 p.m. M-O WATER CARTS inspected by M.O. & Train. Weather FINE	L. 2
	23/9/16		2 H.D. HORSES struck off strength. 1 evacuated from M.V.Secn. & 1 DIED. No. T.S./8483. 4/Farr Cpl. TODD W. 7 o 3. Coy, transferred to 128 F.A. struck off strength & automatically No. 1 Baggage Wagon with "A" Battery 189 Bde. destroyed by Shell fire, reversed 1 "B" " " " " " " " " 1 HQrs Coy move from "BUIRE to BECORDEL. Weather HOTT	L. 1

Army Form C. 2118

WAR DIARY
or
INTELLIGENCE SUMMARY
(Erase heading not required.)

Instructions regarding War Diaries and Intelligence Summaries are contained in F. S. Regs., Part II. and the Staff Manual respectively. Title Pages will be prepared in manuscript.

Place	Date	Hour	Summary of Events and Information	Remarks and references to Appendices
BUIRE	24/9/16		131 Remounts drawn at MERICOURT - await issue to units of Divn. 1 Riding Horse to No Horse received taken on strength. No. T18736 Dr BLOUNT. J. H.A.Coy. (thrown from his wagon) admitted into F.A. struck off strength. Weather Hot	E. J.
	25/9/16		19 Mules drawn at MERICOURT - await issue to units of Divn. Routine Work Weather Hot	E. J.
	26/9/16		Routine Work. 1 Riding Horse left with MAGNIER Victor, BELLOY-SUR-SOMME on bk. cart. H.Q. becoming lame on line of march, cast struck off strength 1 Mule evacuated from M.V. Seen - struck off Weather Hot Baggage Wagons & units of 123rd Infantry Bde. gone their respective units.	E. J.
	27/9/16		1 Mule received from Remounts, taken on strength, issued to H.Q.Coy. Routine Work Weather FINE	E. J.
	28/9/16		No. T2/SR/010149. S.S/M. Cook. J. To H.Coy. evacuated to No.15 CASUALTY CLEARING STATION. No.SY/02098. Pte BARBER C.H.M. H.Qrs Coy / a struck off. Weather DULL - RAIN Routine Work	E. J.

WAR DIARY
or
INTELLIGENCE SUMMARY

(Erase heading not required.)

Army Form C. 2118

Place	Date	Hour	Summary of Events and Information	Remarks and references to Appendices
BUIRE	29/9/16		No 2 Coy move from BUIRE to BECORDEL. Routine Work. Weather RAIN.	Le J
"	30/9/16		Routine Work. a/c HQrs Coy reports that 6.5 wagons reported to be destroyed by shell fire on 23rd inst. "D" Bty, 160 Bde, R.F.A. to be in possession of No 2 Section A.T.C. since returned to HQrs Coy. A report being sent to D.H.Q. accordingly. FAIR & Windy	Le J
	30/9/16			

V.W. Molony, Lieut. Colonel
Commanding 34th Divl. Train. A.S.C.

WAR DIARY
INTELLIGENCE SUMMARY
(Erase heading not required.)

Army Form C. 2118

Place	Date	Hour	Summary of Events and Information	Remarks and references to Appendices
BUIRE.	1/10		Orders received for Divn. HQrs. No 2 & 4 Coys to move to BECORDEL. General Routine Work. Weather fine.	[sig]
"	2/10		Divn. HQrs. No 2 & 4 Coys move to BECORDEL. Orders received for Divn. HQrs. to move to QUARRY. (Ellis) Weather very wet.	[sig]
BECORDEL.	3/10		General Routine Work. Very wet conditions bad for transport work. Weather.	[sig]
"	4/10	9 am	Divn. HQrs. move from BECORDEL to QUARRY (Ellis). 1 H.D. Horse wounded by shrapnel subsequently destroyed. Struck off. 3 " " evacuated to Mobile Veterinary Section. " " No. Jo/065301. Dr GIBBONS F. sent for duty with No. 138 Fd Ambce. Struck off. 2/Lt H.L. HOLLARD ASC to "Y" Corps Rest Station. Weather wet.	[sig]
QUARRY.	5/10		8 wagons on Special Motor Convoy. General Routine. Weather. Much warmer, rain in evening.	[sig]
"	6/10/16		1 H.D. Horse evacuated from Mobile Veterinary Section. Struck off. 2/Lt H.V. CUSACK ASC to M.S. School of Instruction (ST OMER). General Routine. Weather windy.	[sig]

WAR DIARY
INTELLIGENCE SUMMARY
(Erase heading not required.)

Army Form C. 2118

Place	Date	Hour	Summary of Events and Information	Remarks and references to Appendices
QUARRY (Eng)	7/10		2/Lt C.F. LOHNER - 2 Supply Details move to forward area in connection with reserve rations. at slung points. General Routine Work. Weather showery.	[sig]
"	8/10		Pte O FINCH No 2 Coy received slight wounds in ear. General Routine. Weather Dull.	[sig]
"	9/10		General Routine. Weather Dull.	[sig]
"	10/10		138 Remounts arrive at ALBERT for distribution Mobile Veterinary Section taken on strength. Posted to H.Q.Coy. 4 N.T.O. Horses received. General Routine. Weather Fine.	[sig]
"	11/10	9 am	H.Q. Train move to BUIRE. No 2 Coy move from BECORDEL to No E 15 a.B.4.t. 1 Horse evacuated from Mobile Veterinary Section. Struck off. Weather Fine.	[sig]
BUIRE.	12/10/16		General Routine Work. Weather Dull. Warning Orders received for move of Division to North Corps area. Weather fine.	[sig]
	13/10/16		No 3rd Coy move from BECORDEL to BUIRE. Weather fine.	[sig]

WAR DIARY
INTELLIGENCE SUMMARY
(Erase heading not required.)

Army Form C. 2118

Instructions regarding War Diaries and Intelligence Summaries are contained in F. S. Regs., Part II. and the Staff Manual respectively. Title Pages will be prepared in manuscript.

Place	Date	Hour	Summary of Events and Information	Remarks and references to Appendices
BUIRE	14/10	11 am	A.E. GATTIENS. T Train by G.G.L.M. for Dunkirk too. General Routine. Weather Dull.	
"	15/10		General Routine Work. Preparation to move. Weather Dull.	
"	16/10		Train H.Qrs. No. 2 & 4 Coy move together with Transport of Division to ARGOEUVES. No 3 Coy move & billets at ST SAUVIER. Column under command of Lieut. Colonel W.W. Motony. A.C.C. also all billeting arrangements. Weather Fine	
ARGOEUVES	17/10	11 am / 6 pm	Column re-continue march. H.Qr. Train arrive HALLANCOURT - billets there. No 3 Coy Arrive formis await their at queer formis await their tracks to their respective billeting area. Weather. Good of Transport.	
HALLANCOURT	18/10		General Routine. Weather Showery.	
"	19/10	7.41 pm	Part of Train H.Qr. march to ARRAINES - entrain at LONGPRE with No.4 Coy also travel by road arriving at FLETRE @ 4 pm.	
		11.38 pm	No 3 Coy entrain at PONT REMY & detrain at GODEWAERSVELDE - billets in area on 20/10/16. Weather Showery	
FLETRE	20/10	8 am	Part of Train H.Qr. detrain at OMESTRE with No. 4 Coy. & billets at FLETRE.	
		10.11 am	No.3 Coy detrain see 19/10/16.	
			Remainder of Train H.Qr. detachment entrain at LONGPRE @ PONT REMY.	On arrival of No.4 Coy at HAZEBROUCK. 1 Sgt. & 2 N.C.O. Horses missing.
		2.38 pm	No 2 Coy entrain @ PONT REMY	

1875 W.j. W593/326 1,000,000 4/15 J.B.C. & A. A.D.S.S./Forms/C. 2118.

WAR DIARY
INTELLIGENCE SUMMARY

Army Form C. 2118

Place	Date	Hour	Summary of Events and Information	Remarks and references to Appendices
FLETRE	21/10		General Routine. No 4 Coy move from PRINCBOOM to RENINGHELST billets there. Remainder of Train H Qrs detrain at CAESTRE & billet there. No 2 Coy detrain at CAESTRE & billet there. 11 Reinforcements join & taken on strength 1 man evacuated – struck off. Weather fine.	
"	22/10		No 3 Coy move from Billets to RENINGHELST. General Routine. 2nd/Lt H.C. HOLLARD ASC invalided to England & struck off strength. 1 H.D. Horse evacuated & struck off. Weather fine.	
"	23/10		No 7/Hog/223. Dr W. TURNE evacuated to C.C.S. – struck off. Weather fine. Train H Qrs move to RENINGHELST.	
"	24/10		2/Lt C.M.C. LUFF ASC joins from 10th Auxiliary (Horse) Coy (224 Coy) posted to No 2 Coy. No 2 Coy move from CAESTRE to RENINGHELST. General Routine. Weather Rain.	
RENINGHELST	25/10		General Routine. Weather Rain.	
"	26/10			
"	27/10	10 am	No 7518051 O/Cpl Sand Jobson T.E. } No 2 Coy tried by F.G.C.M. at 122 Bde H Qrs No 7515016 " Sand Fry BRADY M. } by MURRAY M. No 7502650 Dr MURRAY M. Weather Rain	

WAR DIARY
INTELLIGENCE SUMMARY
(Erase heading not required.)

Army Form C. 2118

Place	Date	Hour	Summary of Events and Information	Remarks and references to Appendices
RENINGHELST	28/10		8 A/D Horses received from Remounts, taken on strength posted as follows. 2 - No 2 Coy. 5 - No 3 Coy. 1 - H Coy. No T1/09/240. Dr HAINE. F.T. H.QCoy wounded to C.C.S. - struck off. General Routine. Weather wet.	[sig]
	29/10		1 A/D Horse wounded + struck off. No T2/2815.6. Dr GEORGE. A.E. No 2 Coy to 138th F.A. No T3/02/102. Dr HUNTER. P. from 138th F.A. to No 2 Coy. General Routine. Weather wet.	[sig]
	30/10		1/Capt. R.H. KEMP. A.S.C. invalided to England - struck off. 1 A/D Horse H.QCoy destroyed + struck off. No ST A/141. Dr FISHER. G. No 2 Coy to 138th F.A. No T1/0b5299. Dr EVANS O. " " " " No " " " " General Routine. Weather wet.	[sig]
	31/10		General Routine. Weather Very Rough.	[sig]

[signature]
Captain for
Commanding Offr [unit]
Absent on leave

Army Form C. 2118

WAR DIARY
INTELLIGENCE SUMMARY
(Erase heading not required.)

Instructions regarding War Diaries and Intelligence Summaries are contained in F.S. Regs., Part II. and the Staff Manual respectively. Title Pages will be prepared in manuscript.

Place	Date	Hour	Summary of Events and Information	Remarks and references to Appendices
RENINGHELST. Sheet 28. G.31.d central.	1/11/16		General Routine. Weather. Bright during day, rain in evening.	
	2/11/16		F.G.C.M's on S.Sadd. Cpl JOBSON T.E. & Sadd. S¹ BRADY M. promulgated & "Charge "Drunkenness" Sentence. "To be fined £1 (one pound)." No T/1/058109 D² BUTCHER. W.H. No. 4 Coy vacated & struck off. 2 Details join for duty at Divl Boot Repairing Shop. General Routine. Weather. Rain to 9am.	
	3/11/16		Court of Enquiry assembles at Tram H.Qrs regarding 2 Horses No 4 Coy found to be missing from Troops train en route from SOMME to this area. President. Captn Adjt. J.B. WHEATER. A.S.C. Members. Lieut. L.S. LADD A.S.C. 2/Lieut. C.M.C. LUFF. A.S.C. F.G.C.M. D² MURRAY. M. promulgated. Charge "Drunkenness" Sentence:- 3 months F.P. No 1. Fine £1. (one pound) Weather. Dull. General Routine.	
	4/11/16		Visit of DUKE of CONNAUGHT to this area. No. T.3/027003. D² MURRAY M. No 1 Coy died on 1st inst, now struck off strength from that date. No T/1/058109. D² BUTCHER. W.H. No. 2 Coy admitted into Dickebusch Camp. RENINGHELST. WIND. S.S.E. i.e. Very dangerous regarding Gas attacks. Weather. Dull.	

WAR DIARY
INTELLIGENCE SUMMARY
(Erase heading not required.)

Army Form C. 2118

Place	Date	Hour	Summary of Events and Information	Remarks and references to Appendices
RENINGHELST. Sheet 28. G 34 d Central.	5th		1 HD Horse received from Remounts taken on strength posted to No 4 Coy. Manual instruction of Camp etc by O/C Shaw. Convoy of 32 wagons gone for Straw. Weather. Rain.	[signature]
"	6th		Lieut F.A.G.P. GORE. A.S.C. together with 1 Clerk, 1 Interpreter, 1 Motor Car & Driver, proceed to A.S.S.1. 2nd Army for Requisitioning Duties. W.O. Left, visit 4-Cro Coy who are en route for their area from SOMME. Convoy of 30 wagons gone for Straw. Weather Rough wind + rain.	[signature]
"	7th		No 12/1/196. Pt LAWLEY. P, evacuated to C.C.S. — struck off. General Routine. Weather. Heavy Rain.	[signature]
"	8th		No 1/30/51, Pt CLARKSON. J. returned from H.Qrs, 2nd Army, taken on strength posted to 4-Cro Coy. 1. Captain. G.H. COLEGRAVE. A.S.C. join formation from 1st Army (Aux) Horse Coy (425 Coy. H.S.C.) — taken on strength, posted to 4-Cro Coy. Weather Rain. General Routine.	[signature]
"	9th		1. Capt: COLEGRAVE. G.H. A.S.C. join Horse Train from 1st Army Aux (Horse) Coy, (425 Coy) posted to 4-Cro Coy. 2. Details evacuated, struck off strength. No 1/31238. A/Sadn. S. Sgt Nolan. G. No 4 Coy, evacuated to C.C.S on 1st inst, struck off. No 34/110341. Pt Grinch. O. No 2 Coy, evacuated to C.C.S. on 1st inst, struck off.	[signature]

Army Form C. 2118

WAR DIARY
or
INTELLIGENCE SUMMARY
(Erase heading not required.)

Instructions regarding War Diaries and Intelligence Summaries are contained in F.S. Regs., Part II. and the Staff Manual respectively. Title Pages will be prepared in manuscript.

Place	Date	Hour	Summary of Events and Information	Remarks and references to Appendices
RENINGHELST Sheet 28. G 34 d central	10/11/16		1 MD Horse "Ho No Coy destroyed by Shrapnel on 30/10/16, now struck off. 2 2nd Lt C.F. LOCHNER. A.S.C. proceeds to Ho Qrs 2nd Army in connection with Requisitioning Duties vice Lieut F.A.G.P. GOTE. A.S.C. who rejoins formation. Weather Fine. General Routine.	[signature]
	11/11/16		No TH/058109 A/ BUTCHER W.H. No No Coy from Divl Rect Station. Lieut F.A.G.P. GOTE A.S.C. to 60th. Divl Train. H Qr Coy arrive in this area encamp at G 32 d 8.8. No T3/026944-2. A/ GATIENS. T to Aldershot Camp. RENINGHELST. Weather fine. General Routine.	[signature]
		5 pm		
	12/11/16		10 Remounts Received posted to HQrs Coy. 1 MD Horse destroyed 29/10/16 now struck off. No TS/8275. Van Dr COPPING. G.C. HQrs Coy died in No6 Stationary H. on 6th inst, now struck off. Weather fine. General Routine.	[signature]
	13/11/16		No T3/026891 Dr PICKERGILL. C.A. No 3 Coy evacuated to C.C.S. now struck off. Transports as Usual Routine. Weather. FINE.	[signature]

WAR DIARY
INTELLIGENCE SUMMARY

(Erase heading not required.)

Army Form C. 2118

Instructions regarding War Diaries and Intelligence Summaries are contained in F. S. Regs., Part II. and the Staff Manual respectively. Title Pages will be prepared in manuscript.

Place	Date	Hour	Summary of Events and Information	Remarks and references to Appendices
RENINGHELST Sheet 28 G 31 a central	14/1/16		WIND DANGEROUS. ORDERED 1 Remount Received horses to Rest Coy. General Routine. Weather FINE	
	15/1/16		General Routine. Weather Fine.	
	16/1/16		No. 4 Coy off duty this day in respect of Transport, whole day devoted to General Drill, also horse + inspection, also camp improvements carried out. Transport (supply) provided for Rest Coy from remaining Coys. Weather Dry. Very Cold. 9 HD Horses from HQ Coy A.O.C. visits No. 21 Coy camp. sent to M.V.S. for evacuation. struck off strength	
	17/1/16		No. 3 Coy off duty for Training Drills. 1 HD HQ Coy Cpl. struck off. Dr LAWLER P. rejoins HQ Coy from C.C.S. Dr JOHNSON.H. " " " Weather Dry. VERY COLD.	

Army Form C. 2118

WAR DIARY
INTELLIGENCE SUMMARY
(Erase heading not required.)

Instructions regarding War Diaries and Intelligence Summaries are contained in F.S. Regs., Part II. and the Staff Manual respectively. Title Pages will be prepared in manuscript.

Place	Date	Hour	Summary of Events and Information	Remarks and references to Appendices
RENINGHELST Sheet 28 Q.34 Central	18/9/16		C.O. inspects 1st Line transport of 122 Infy Bde. General routine carry-on. Weather cold – much rain	[initials]
	19/9/16		General routine. Weather wet.	[initials]
	20/9/16		General routine. Capt. W.H. SHEFFIELD, R.A.M.C. took on medical charge vice T/Capt. E.S. MOORHEAD. T/Lieut H. MORRIS A.S.C. to be T/Capt. from 17th SEPTEMBER 1916. 1. H.Q. Horse (Head Groom) left at VILLERS BOCAGE struck off strength. Weather fine.	[initials]
	21/9/16		Refilling from pack train direct at WIPPENHOEK. Refilling dumps abolished. General routine. Weather fine.	[initials]
	22/9/16		F.G.C.M. on A/Sgt CHURCHILL No.1 Coy — adjourned till 23rd inst.	[initials]
	23/9/16		General routine. Weather fine.	[initials]
	24/9/16		General routine. Weather fine. 1. Riding Horse (No.3), No.2 Coy destroyed – struck off strength.	[initials]
	25/9/16		Supply detail of all companies quartered in huts at SONNAUGHT LINES, WIPPENHOEK SIDING from to-day inclusive. 47 Mahe in charge weather wet. One Pack charge Welsh Coy destroyed – struck off. General routine.	[initials]

F.G.C.M. = Dr BODLEY G. No 2 Coy.

WAR DIARY or INTELLIGENCE SUMMARY

Army Form C. 2118

Place	Date	Hour	Summary of Events and Information	Remarks and references to Appendices
RENINGHELST Sheet 28 G 34 Central	26/11		General Routine. F.G.C.M. on 2/Sgt CHURCHILL W.A.M. promulgated. Charge (1) Disobeying a lawful command. (2) An act to the prejudice of good order military discipline gaol a wrong tale when on our escort duties to Locreie. (1) NOT GUILTY. (11) GUILTY. Sentence. Deprived of 2/Rank and Deprivage 2 months F.P. No.1. Weather fine.	[signature]
	27/11		C.O. inspected 1st Line Transport of 1,2,3 2/4 Bdes. General routine. Weather fine.	[signature]
	28/11		General routine. Weather fine.	[signature]
	29/11		General routine. Weather foggy. Reinforcements from Base:- T/9697 Sgt Scarratt, T/37175 W Seth Carrill, T/431803 Dr Barley, T/030751 Dr Le Marchant, T/33202 Dr Horn + T/440634 Dr Hughes. 1 H.S. Horse on charge No. 4 Coy. destroyed stick of strength.	[signature]
	30/11		General routine. F.G.C.M. on Pte BODLEY G No2 Coy promulgated. Charge "Using insubordinate language to his superior officer" SENTENCE 35 days F.P. No. II. Pte CONYERS W. admitted into detention camp RENINGHURST. Weather fine.	[signature]

[signature]
Capt. R.
for CMDG. 41st DIVNL. TRAIN, A.S.C.

Army Form C. 2118

WAR DIARY

INTELLIGENCE SUMMARY

(Erase heading not required.)

Instructions regarding War Diaries and Intelligence Summaries are contained in F.S. Regs., Part II. and the Staff Manual respectively. Title Pages will be prepared in manuscript.

Place	Date	Hour	Summary of Events and Information	Remarks and references to Appendices
RENINGHELST Sheet 28 G.34.d central	1/12/16		G.O.C. 41st Division permits the sentence of 2 months F.P. No.1 in the case of Pte. (A/Sgt) Churchill tried by F.G.C.M. on the 22nd–24th NOVEMBER, 1916. General routine. Weather fine, very cold.	[signature]
	2/12/16		General routine. Two Riding Transport fAn. by. 1 to 52nd Mot Vet Section struck off strength & struck off strength (" 1 to " , 1 to 10 in Queen. Weather fine, very cold.	[signature]
	3/12/16		6 A.V. Horses received from Remounts, taken on strength posted to HQrs Company. General Routine. Weather Dull.	[signature]
	4/12/16		2 A.V. Horses ThereLy evacuated from 52nd Mobile Veterinary Section struck off strength. Inspection of Transport of 138th Field Ambulance by O/C Train. General Routine. Weather fine.	[signature]
	5/12/16		Inspection of Transport of 139 Field Ambulance by O/C Train. " " " 2 Units 123rd Infantry Bde by O/C Train. No. T2/13212. Sgt. (A/CSM) Spouse R, No.2 Coy tried by F.G.C.M. charge "Drunkenness". Weather Rain.	[signature]
	6/12/16		Inspection of Transport of 140 Field Ambulance by O/C Train. J.A.Coy. on A/CSM. SPOUSE R promulgated. Sentence of Court was "To forfeit 6 months seniority as regards his permanent grade as Sergeant & A/Sgt SPOUSE R No.2 Coy reverts to permanent grade of Sergeant. 1 Driver joins Train posted to HQrs Coy.	[signature]

1875 Wt. W593/826 1,000,000 4/15 J.B.C. & A. A.D.S.S./Forms/C. 2118.

Army Form C. 2118

WAR DIARY
INTELLIGENCE SUMMARY
(Erase heading not required.)

Instructions regarding War Diaries and Intelligence Summaries are contained in F.S. Regs., Part II. and the Staff Manual respectively. Title Pages will be prepared in manuscript.

Place	Date	Hour	Summary of Events and Information	Remarks and references to Appendices
RENINGHELST (Sheet 28) (G.3.d.Central)	7/12/16		3 drivers evacuated & struck off strength. General Routine.	
	8/12/16		Transport of 10th Middlesex (Pioneers) Regt inspected by O/C Train. 1 driver evacuated & struck off strength. General Routine.	
	9/12/16	3 pm	12 remounts arrive at HOPPOUTRE — received by O/C Train to ride.	
			5 remounts received from Remounts, taken on strength & posted to Ho Qrs Coy. General Routine. Weather mild.	
	10/12/16		1 N.C.O. & 1 man evacuated & struck off strength. 1 man (Pioneer Battn.) joins for course of instruction in cold shoeing. General Routine.	
	11/12/16		1 N.C.O. evacuated & struck off General Routine. 1 2nd Lieut. H.T. Cusack A.S.C. struck off strength.	
	12/12/16		Transport as usual. 1 Captain R.P. REDMAN. A.S.C. evacuated to C.C.S. suffering from Broken leg.	
	13/12/16		1 Captn. G.H. COLEGRAVE. A.S.C. posted to Command No.1 Coy. 1 Lieut. C. TRIPP. A.S.C. from No.2 Coy to H.Qrs Coy. 1 2/Lt. H.N. PAGE. A.S.C. from H.Qrs Coy to No.2 Coy. General Routine.	

Army Form C. 2118

WAR DIARY
INTELLIGENCE SUMMARY
(Erase heading not required.)

Instructions regarding War Diaries and Intelligence Summaries are contained in F.S. Regs., Part II. and the Staff Manual respectively. Title Pages will be prepared in manuscript.

Place	Date	Hour	Summary of Events and Information	Remarks and references to Appendices
Reninghelst Sheet 28 G 3 d central	14/12/16		General Routine. Mules & wagons detailed for R.E. services at R.E. Dump.	
	15/12/16		General Routine.	
	16/12/16		1 Man going for temporary duty (with base No 17719) General Routine.	
	17/12/16		1 Man going from Base Depot to posted to HqrCoy General Routine	
	18/12/16		Guns of refilling changes at Railhead, transport to be at that place at 9.30 a.m. General Transport Routine. 2,104 Mules transport Stores of 123 Infantry Bde relieved by 2 Divn No 3 Coy Spare	
	19/12/16		Routine as usual	
	20/12/16		Mules 8 wagons detailed for duty at R.E. Dump. General Routine.	
	21/12/16		1 Driver struck off strength. admitted the Divl Detention Camp. General Transport Routine.	
	22/12/16		General Routine. 8 wagons placed at disposal of NCOs	

1875 Wt. W593/826 1,000,000 4/15 J.B.C. & A. A.D.S.S./Forms/C. 2118.

WAR DIARY
INTELLIGENCE SUMMARY
(Erase heading not required.)

Army Form C. 2118

Place	Date	Hour	Summary of Events and Information	Remarks and references to Appendices
RENINGHELST Sheet 28 G 34 d central	23/12/16		General Routine. 8 wagons for R.E's. Strong Gale. Blows.	[sig]
	24/12/16		10 wagons for Straw. 8 " " R.E's. Transport Routine as usual.	[sig]
	25/12/16		Commander-in-Chief Army Comdr. Corps Comdr. Divl. Comdr., sent their Xmas Xmas Year greetings to all ranks. Supplies delayed for about 2 hours owing to late arrival of train at Rhine. General Routine.	[sig]
	26/12/16		G.O.C. inspects all horses of this formation. 1 N.C.O. joins train, taken on strength. Posted to No 3 Coy 8 wagons for R.E's Transport as usual	[sig]
	27/12/16		1 Capt R. P. REDMAN A.S.C invalided to England, struck off strength. 1 man purceded to England for temporary commission in Infantry, struck off. General Routine.	[sig]
	28/12/16		12 Almonds arrive at WIPPENHOEK, for distribution to units of Division. 8 wagons for R.E's parties. Transport the usual.	[sig]

WAR DIARY
INTELLIGENCE SUMMARY
(Erase heading not required.)

Army Form C. 2118

Place	Date	Hour	Summary of Events and Information	Remarks and references to Appendices
RENINGHELST Sheet 28 G 34 central	29/12/16		4 H.O. Horses, 7 1 A.S. Mules, M.Qr.Coy. encountes from 52 Mobile Veterinary Section - struck off strength taken on strength as follows:- 3 N.O. Horses & 1 L.D. Mule received from remounts, No 2 Coy HQrs Coy 1 A.S. Horse, 1 L.D. Mule. 1 L.D. Horse General Transport Routine.	
	30/12/16		S/Captn M.B. POLLARD-URGUHART. A.S.C. joins from 39th Divl Train. 1 N.C.O. joins from base, & posted to No 1 Coy. 1 Horse No 3 Coy destroyed. Transport as usual.	
	31/12/16		1 N.C.O. transferred to Base, as surplus to establishment, & so struck off. 8 Gunners for R.G.A. work. Transport as usual.	

COMMDG. 41st DIVNL. TRAIN, A.S.C.

Army Form C. 2118

WAR DIARY
or
INTELLIGENCE SUMMARY
(Erase heading not required.)

41st DIVNL. TRAIN, A.S.C.

Instructions regarding War Diaries and Intelligence Summaries are contained in F.S. Regs., Part II. and the Staff Manual respectively. Title Pages will be prepared in manuscript.

Place	Date	Hour	Summary of Events and Information	Remarks and references to Appendices
RENINGHELST. Sheet 28 G.3.d Central.	1/1/17	10 a.m.	T/4/057512. Dr WALLACE. T. H.Qrs Coy tried by G.C.M. at H.Qrs Coy "Drunkenness" TS/8125. Wkr D/E.C. WEST. No 3 Coy released from Divl. Detention Camp. General Routine.	JBC
	2/1/17		1/AD. Morris in charge of H.Qrs Coy destroyed & struck off strength T/2 Coy "off Duty" for general cleaning of company lines etc etc. General Routine.	JBC
	3/1/17	5 pm	T/2/10163. Dr KELLY. J.J. H.QrsCoy admitted to Divl. Detention Camp. General Routine.	JBC
	4/1/17		Lieut Colonel W.W. MOLONY A.S.C. granted 21 days leave. Major. P.W. PROCKTER A.S.C. Assumes command of Divl. Train. 3 men released from Divl. Detention Camp. Sentence on T/4/057512. D/r WALLACE. T. H.QrsCoy promulgated. 120 days Imprisonment, hard labour.	JBC
	5/1/17		General Routine.	JBC
	6/1/17		General Routine.	JBC
	7/1/17		No T/4/09/4210. D/r PEARCE. A.J. H.Qrs Coy evacuated & struck off strength. No T/4/062033 D/r COX.J. ~ T/T/020085 General Routine. Sad/r STEVENS. wounded by shrapnel fire, struck off strength	JBC
	8/1/17		Comp. Instructors, Boot-house fitting & Cupbuildings by Divl. Boot Repairing Shop. 1 man going for duty in Divl. Boot Repairing Shop.	JBC

Army Form C. 2118

WAR DIARY
or
INTELLIGENCE SUMMARY
(Erase heading not required.)

Place	Date	Hour	Summary of Events and Information	Remarks and references to Appendices
REMINGHELST SHEET 28 G3.d. central	9/7		Sentences of 120 days I.H.L. passed upon T/4/057512 Dr WALLACE. T. H.Qrs Coy, now reduced to read " 30 days F.P.No1. (authority H.Q.1st Divn "1/9 a.56/299 A/9/7")	BQ
		5pm	No. T/4/057512. D' WALLACE. T. H.Qrs Coy admitted to Divl. Detention Camp. No. T/3/026953. C.S.M. MACKENZIE. E. No 3 Coy. released for Temporary Infantry. Commission. proceeded this day, + struck off strength to England. No T/4/06524?. A/S' MORRIS. F. No 3 Coy evacuated sick - struck off	BQ
	10/7		Transport detailed at Railhead owing to late arrival of pack train. 53 Remounts received, taken on strength. + posted as follow: H.Qrs Coy No.2 Coy. No.3 Coy 23, 5, 1, 1	BQ
	11/7		No A530. D' MOORE. A.S. H.Qrs Coy evacuated sick - struck off No T/4/054065+. D' WAITE. E.A " " " " " Transport Routine as usual.	BQ BQ
	12/7		General Routine.	BQ
	13/7		Nothing to report.	BQ
	14/7		1 H.O. "Horse No Coy died, + struck off 1 Mule " " No 3 Coy " " " " General Routine.	BQ
	15/7		No T/4/094352. Dr WATSON W. " T/1/6515 " Mc LOCKLAND. M. Join from A.D.C. Base Depot (A.I.-I) taken on " T/6/611 " ASHWIN. J. strength + posted to H.Qrs Coy	BQ

Army Form C. 2118

WAR DIARY
or
INTELLIGENCE SUMMARY
(Erase heading not required.)

Instructions regarding War Diaries and Intelligence Summaries are contained in F.S. Regs, Part II. and the Staff Manual respectively. Title Pages will be prepared in manuscript.

Place	Date	Hour	Summary of Events and Information	Remarks and references to Appendices
RENINGHELST Sheet 28 G.34.d central	16/1/17		No 72/10863. Dr KELLY. J.J. HQ+CoY relieves from Detention Camp & returned to duty. General Routine.	[signature]
	17/1/17		General Routine.	[signature]
	18/1/17		T/34237. A/FARR ROBERTS. C, HQ+Coy, evacuated to Base as "surplus to establishment. T/400+222. D/CROOKER. E. HQ+Coy evacuated to CCS. - struck off. Transport on march.	[signature]
	19/1/17		T/5/5488 A/Saw Corpl. USHER T. } HQ+Coy evacuated to CCS & struck off T/3/0290 Hb A/Cpl MEADOWS. C } General Routine.	[signature]
	20/1/17		T/4/04.4263, Sgt HOOKS. G.H. No 3 Coy, to England for Commission. Supplies refilled at Railhead @ 7 am.	[signature]
	21/1/17		T/4/06524-7. A/MORRIS. F. No 3. struck off on 20/1/17 rejoins No 3 Coy for duty & reinforcements from train from Base Depot, taken on strength & posted as follows. 1 to 138 F.A. — 1 to 139 F.A. — 2 to 140 F.A. General Routine.	[signature]
	22/1/17		1 H.Q. Horse HQ+Coy evacuated & struck off General Routine.	[signature]

WAR DIARY
or
INTELLIGENCE SUMMARY
(Erase heading not required.)

Army Form C. 2118

Place	Date	Hour	Summary of Events and Information	Remarks and references to Appendices
Renninghelen Sheet 28 & 34 d central	23/7		General Routine.	
	24/7		13/02/003. Lt MURRAY. M. No 2 Coy released from Five Detention Camp, & returned to General Routine. Given horse remounted to Mobile Vet. Section.	
	25/7		No. T4/108200 Dr Smart J.W. Hd Qtr Coy. remounted to E.C.S. Struck off. Lieut Colonel WOLO Malony resumed command of 41st Divl Train. General Routine	
	26/7		General Routine.	
	27/7		No. T4/094222 Dr Crocker E. Hd Qtr Co. Rejoins from E.C.S. Taken on strength. No. T4/069687 Dr Sellstone R. Joins from duty. Posted to Hd Qtr Co. Remainder routine as usual.	
	28/7		General routine.	
	29/7		General routine.	
	30/7		Dvr H.D. Howe on charge H.Qrs Coy. died struck off. No. T/7659 Dr Lindal L. 2 Coy. admitted into Divl Detention Camp. No. T4/087752 Dr Wallace T. Hd Qr Coy. discharged fm Divl Detention Camp General routine	
	31/7		General routine.	

J.B. ... Lt. Col.
Commdg 41st Divnl Train, A.S.C.

WAR DIARY
or
INTELLIGENCE SUMMARY

(Erase heading not required.)

Army Form C. 2118

Place	Date	Hour	Summary of Events and Information	Remarks and references to Appendices
RENINGHELST Sht 28 G.3.H.1 Central	1/7/17		General Routine	
	2/7/17		General Routine	
	3/7/17		No. T030751 Dr Le Marchand A.W. No 2 Coy. proceeded to Fd. Ots for duty vice Lt. Col. of Manual Routine	
	4/7/17		No. S4/064854 A/g. Sgt Ward J.J. No.2 Coy. proceeded to England to take up Temp. Commission & struck off strength. General routine	
	5/7/17		General routine	
	6/7/17		Six Orderly N.C.O's appointed L/Cpls. General routine	
	7/7/17		No. T/15375 Dr McLoughlin M. Fd. Otr Coy. transferred to C.C.S. struck off strength. General Routine	
	8/7/17		General Routine	
	9/7/17		No. T/24017 A/Cpl Beard J. Fd. Ofr Coy. evacuated to C.C.S. No. T/2109 Dr Hallett G. Fd. Ofr Coy. struck off strength. No. T/SR 03773 Dr Wood A.E. rejoined from 52nd Mobile Vet Section, taken on strength to No. 2 Coy. 11 H.Q. Horses & 1 mule received Reinforcements taken on strength. General Routine	

WAR DIARY
or
INTELLIGENCE SUMMARY

(Erase heading not required.)

Army Form C. 2118

Instructions regarding War Diaries and Intelligence Summaries are contained in F. S. Regs., Part II. and the Staff Manual respectively. Title Pages will be prepared in manuscript.

Place	Date	Hour	Summary of Events and Information	Remarks and references to Appendices
RENINGHELST Sheet 28 G.3.d Central	10/2/17		General Routine	[signature]
	11/2/17		General Routine	[signature]
	12/2/17		C.O. inspects 1st Line Transport 12 M Role. General routine	[signature]
	13/2/17		No. T364551 A/Corporal No.1 Coy. No. T32536 A/L/Sgt Bridgey A. No. 2 Coy. + SW/707722 Pte Satterthwaite G. No. 2 Coy appointed U/Cpls with pay. SW/059673 Cpl Gordon H. No. 3 Coy appointed A/S/Sgt with pay from S-Sgt. General Routine	[signature]
	14/2/17		General routine. Lieut A.S. Black No.1 Coy placed on sick list.	[signature]
	15/2/17		No. T24017 A/Sgt Bend J. No.1 Coy rejoined from C.C.S. is taken on the strength. General routine	[signature]
	16/2/17		General routine	[signature]
	17/2/17		No. T6575 Pte McLoughlin M. No.1 Coy rejoined from C.C.S. is taken on the strength. No. T36591 Pte Davie W. No.2 Coy evacuated to 3rd Canadian C.C.S. is struck off the strength. General routine. Divisional Commander inspects Nos 2 & 3 Coys.	[signature]

Army Form C. 2118

WAR DIARY
or
INTELLIGENCE SUMMARY
(Erase heading not required.)

Instructions regarding War Diaries and Intelligence Summaries are contained in F.S. Regs., Part II. and the Staff Manual respectively. Title Pages will be prepared in manuscript.

Place	Date	Hour	Summary of Events and Information	Remarks and references to Appendices
RENINGHELST Sheet 28. G 3 & 4 Central.	18/2/17		General routine. Divisional Commander inspects No. 4 Coy.	[signature]
	19/2/17		Divisional Commander inspects Helgrants Coy. S.R.E. Postal Section attached Hd Qtrs No. 59839 Cpl Main No. 36078 Pioneer Bowling transferred to B.T.R.S. on 11 Wmd. No. 29213 Sgt Allen of W. Coy No. 5092 Sapr. Patterson R.E. Postal Section joined on the strength attached to Hd Qrs Coy. One H.29 Horse No. 103 in large Hd Qrs Coy cast/casualty struck off. Usual routine. Lieut W.S. Meik, 3 Coy, placed on Sick List.	[signature]
	20/2/17		Usual routine. Refilling at WIPPENHOEK commenced 10 am	[signature]
	21/2/17		General routine.	[signature]
	22/2/17		One H.29 Horse received from Remounts, taken on strength posted to 3 Coy. General routine. No. T/65172 2/Lt THORPE A. Hd Qtrs Coy admitted to Hospital self inflicted.	[signature]
	23/2/17		No. T/3700 2/Lt Cpl Entwistle J.H. No. T/35395 2/Lt Walden A. No. 3 Coy. having been sentenced to C.C.S. in 11d & 17 days respectively are struck off strength. Four reinforcements join from Base H.J.S Depot. General routine.	[signature]

WAR DIARY or INTELLIGENCE SUMMARY

Army Form C. 2118

(Erase heading not required.)

Place	Date	Hour	Summary of Events and Information	Remarks and references to Appendices
RENINGHELST Sheet 28 C.34.d Central	24/7/17		No. T.S. 8961 A/S.S.M./S/Sgt. Dickenson J.G. Hd-Qr. Coy. reverts to permanent grade of Dvr. at his own request from this day inclusive. General routine.	
	25/7/17		No. S4/064854 A/S.S. Major J.J. reverts to permanent grade of Sgt. in reversion to England for General routine.	
	26/7/17		The following 2nd Line Transport transferred from No.1 Coy. to 2nd Army Field Artillery Schl. for administration. Horses H.D. 32. Wagons G.S. Hd. × 16. Driver 16. Strength off strength of their formation from 27 this inclusive. No. S4/044403 A/Sgt. Jackson and No 3 Coy. appointed A/S.Sgt. with pay. No. T/1659 Dr Linda L. No. 3 Coy. released from Div. Detention Camp this day. General Routine.	
	27/7/17		One H.Q.Horse in charge Hd.Qr. Coy. died on 26 inst. in strength off strength. Lieut A.B. Black returned to duty 26 inst., is taken off Rect. List. Capt. Wyttigan, 12 Bd. E. Surrey Regt. joined for course of instruction & on instruction removed from midnight tonight. General routine.	
	28/7/17		General Routine.	

J.B. Peake
Capt for Commdg 41st Divl Train.

WAR DIARY or INTELLIGENCE SUMMARY

Army Form C. 2118

Place	Date	Hour	Summary of Events and Information	Remarks and references to Appendices
RENINGHELST Sheet 28 G 34 d. central	1/3/17		In accordance with new War Estab, the following detail in Transport to Train H.Q.R :- Capt. G.M.C. Ruttle from 1 Coy, 2 Lt. G.M.C. Luff from 2 Coy, 10 O/R from 1 Coy, 1 O/R from 2 Coy, 3 O/R from 3 Coy, 2 Ptes from 4 Coy. — T/8578 W/Sgt Wooper G.S. from No. 1 Coy to 4 Coy + T/022987 W/Sgt. Ball W. from No. 3 Coy to No. 2 Coy. L.S.G.M. of No. T/023752 Dr. T. Tate. No. 1 Coy. Capt. D.J. Galbraith proceeds General routine. Lieut. W.S. Meade with 8 duty Take off civil lors.	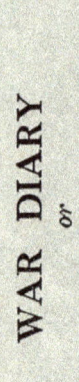
	2/3/17		No. T/5/8966 Dr. S.H. Brady. M. No. 2 Coy. evacuated to C.C.S. 26th attack off. Two H.D. Horses evacuated to 52nd Mob. Vet. Section attack off. General Routine.	
	3/3/17		No. 10899 Pte Heinri G. 122 m. G. Coy + No. 2237 Pte Tone J. L. Coy 19th Middlesex Regt having completed a course of Cobral Shoeing returned to duty sent on 24 or 2 7th inspected. General Routine. No. T/86501 Dr. Moore 67. No.3 Coy evacuated to No. 15 66 C.S. sick Notorial	
	4/3/17		The following detail (complete to establishment) transferred to the Advanced H.Q. Depot from No. 6 Coy. Strike off the strength. 5. Driver. 10. H. & Horses. 8 wagons G.S. Limble act of harness. General routine.	
	5/3/17		General Routine.	
	6/3/17		General Routine.	

Army Form C. 2118

WAR DIARY
or
INTELLIGENCE SUMMARY
(Erase heading not required.)

Instructions regarding War Diaries and Intelligence Summaries are contained in F. S. Regs., Part II. and the Staff Manual respectively. Title Pages will be prepared in manuscript.

Place	Date	Hour	Summary of Events and Information	Remarks and references to Appendices
RENINGHELST Sheet 28 G.N. of Central	7/3/17		General Routine. No. T/030708 N Swan W. Rout Cy admitted into Divl. Dentention Camp on 1st inst. discharged from Divl. Detention Camp this day returned to duty with 4 Cy a Draw.	
	8/3/17		General Routine. Capt Cottages 12 with E. Surrey Regt. completed course of instruction, Sgst of	
	9/3/17		General Routine. No. T/35659 N Hyam L.W., No. 3. Cy. & No. T.5/8365 N Fanfushing R.W. No. 4 Cy. evacuated to C.C.S. on 3rd inst returned of midnight.	
	10/3/17		No. T/065205 D. Mellerd H.q. No. 3 Cy. admitted into Divl. Dentention Camp. on 3rd inst. discharged from Divl. Detention Camp this day returned to duty with 3 Cy a Draw. No. T/623752 N TATE. T. No. 1 Cy. Promulgated. Charge 1. Gave a name other than his own with intention to deceive. Charge 2. Wilfully galloped a H.D. Horse whilst in a lame condition. Charge 3. Galloped a pair of H.D. Horses coming to a water trotting canter. Sentence. 56 Days F.P. No. 1.	
	11/3/17		General Routine. No. T/3/023752 N Tate T. No 1 Cy. admitted into Divl. Detention Camp. General Routine.	
	12/3/17		One Rly. Horse in charge No 3 Cy. evacuated Sgst of A.G.G.H. on 7th /058712 D THORPE A. No 1 Cy. charge: Conduct to the prejudice of good order & military discipline (carelessly wounding himself in the left foot) Accused was found guilty & awarded 28 days F.P. No. 1. General Routine.	

1875 Wt. W593/826 1,000,000 4/15 J.B.C. & A. A.D.S.S./Forms/C. 2118.

WAR DIARY or INTELLIGENCE SUMMARY

(Erase heading not required.)

Army Form C. 2118

Place	Date	Hour	Summary of Events and Information	Remarks and references to Appendices
RENINGHELST Sheet 28 r G 34 d Central	13/3/17		One H.D. Horse on charge No.1 Coy, died this day, struck off. General routine.	
	14/3/17		No. 54/04390? Pte Collard H.E. No.3 Coy. admitted into Divl. Detention Camp. General routine.	
	15/3/17		General routine. 26 Horses recd. from 187th Bde R.F.A. suspected suffering from MANGE. Capt. W.B. Pollard Urquhart placed on Sick list.	
	16/3/17		One H.D. Horse on charge No.4 Coy. destroyed. Struck off. General routine.	
	17/3/17		No. T4/058084 2/ SPARROW. A.V.R. No.2 Coy proceeded to England to take up a temporary commission. Struck off. No. T4/094029 2/ PARRETT G.C. No.1 Coy. evacuated to C.C.S. on 11th inst. Struck off. 2nd Lt. A.N. PAGE. A.S.C. struck off strength from 8th inst. C.O. suspects No 3 Coy.	
	18/3/17		No. R/10947 Rfn ADAMS A. 18th Bttn K.R.R. Corps joined to undergo course of instruction in Cold Shoeing, attached to 2 Coy. General routine.	
	19/3/17		General Routine. Capt. W.B. POLLARD URQUHART. No.1 Coy returned to duty. Taken off sick list. 26 Horses recd. from 187th Bde RFA. stopped for Mange.	

1875 Wt. W 593/826 1,000,000 4/15 J.B.C. & A. A.D.S.S./Forms/C. 2118.

WAR DIARY
or
INTELLIGENCE SUMMARY
(Erase heading not required.)

Army Form C. 2118

Place	Date	Hour	Summary of Events and Information	Remarks and references to Appendices
RENINGHELST Sheet 28 G.24.d Central	20/3/17		25 Transport N.C.O's confirmed in rank } Authority A.S.C. Section P4/1531/71 d/15/3/17. 15 Supply N.C.O's confirmed in rank 15 Reinforcements form from Base Depot (ATTS). Posted as follows:- 3 to 186 F.Amb. 3 to 139th F.Amb., 3 to 140th F.Amb., 3 to No. 2 Coy + 3 to No. 3 of Train. General Routine. C.O. inspected 12 Lorries + part of 122 Stable.	[signature]
	21/3/17		Board assembled at Train Hd. Qtr @ 11 a.m. to report upon a consignment of Supplies as to their fitness for consumption. President Major J.T. BEADLE, 11th R.W. KENT Regt. Member { Capt. L.S. LADD A.S.C. 2/L. C.M.C. LUFF A.S.C. General Routine.	[signature]
	22/3/17		No. T4/057476 A/C.S.M. RILEY P.S. No. 1 Coy. } Confirmed in their rank (W.O. class II). No. T2/S.R. 01405 A/C.S.M. WIGSTON T. No.4 Coy.} Authority A.S.C. Records Woolwich Dkyard. No. C.R./7884/C/116 d/10/3/17 + A.S.C. Section at Base P7/25/41. General Routine. No 4 Coy moves to STEENVOORDE AREA.	[signature]
	23/3/17		General Routine.	[signature]
	24/3/17		Summer Time adopted @ 11p.m. all clocks advanced one hour.	[signature]

War Diary or Intelligence Summary

Army Form C. 2118

Place	Date	Hour	Summary of Events and Information	Remarks and references to Appendices
RENINGHELST Shed 28 G.B.H.D. Central.	25/3/17		31 N.C.O.'s & Men of Hd Qts: & No. 1 Coy. awarded 1st G.C. Badge. General Routine	
	26/3/17		21 N.C.O.'s & Men of No. 2 Coy. awarded 1st G.C. Badge. 1/2nd Lieut. G. WARRINGTON A.S.C. joined from 8th AUX (HORSE) Coy. ROUEN, posted to 4 Coy. General Routine	
	27/3/17		19 N.C.O.'s Pros. of No. 3 Coy. awarded 1st G.C. Badge. Extract from LONDON Gazette 27/3/17. Lieut. H. MORRIS to be T/CAPTAIN from 27/2/17. No. 043902 Pte COLLARD H.C. No. 3 Coy. discharged from Duke Station Camp. General Routine.	
	28/3/17		20 N.C.O.'s & Men of No. 4 Coy. awarded 1st G.C. Badge. 3 Reinforcements from Base H.T.I.S. Depot joined. General Routine	
	29/3/17		One N.C.O. & Men of Train Hd Qts. awarded 1st G.C. Badge. General Routine. Capt. V.H. PENNELL No. 1 Coy. Placed on Staff List.	
	30/3/17		One H.B.Horse No. 47 in charge of Coy. detachment 29 Bum. & 7 H.D.Horse No. 117 in reinforcement to 52 Br. V. Section. 29 Buns. are struck off strength.	
	31/3/17		Capt. W.H. SHEFFIELD R.A.M.C. proceeded to England on expiration of Contract. Struck off strength. Capt. Reg. Horse in charge C. joined vice Capt. W.H. SHEFFIELD R.A.M.C. taken on strength. One H.B.Horse No. 41 in charge No. 3 Coy. reinforcement 28 Bum. struck off. General Routine	

WAR DIARY or INTELLIGENCE SUMMARY

Army Form C. 2118

Place	Date	Hour	Summary of Events and Information	Remarks and references to Appendices
RENINGHELST Sheet 28. G 3 H. d. Central	1/4/17		8 Reinforcements join from Base H.T.T.S. Depot. General Routine.	
	2/4/17		8 N.C.O's proceeded to course of instruction at Divl. Gas School. General Routine. No. T/4/86501 Dr MOORE E.F. rejoined from No. 15. C.C.S. taken on strength. No. T/4/108165 L/CPL OSBORNE No. 1 Cy. evacuated to C.C.S struck off.	
	3/4/17		One H.Q. Horse killed & H.Q. Horse wounded by shell fire. On charge No. 1. Cy. General routine. One H.Q. Horse on charge No. 2 Cy. evacuated 3rd strength of.	
	4/4/17		No. T/36591 Dr DAVIES R.W. No. 2 Coy. rejoined from 3rd C.C.S. Station, taken on strength. General routine.	
	5/4/17		8 N.C.O's rejoin, having completed a course of instruction at Divl. Gas School. General Routine.	
	6/4/17		No. 4 Coy return from STEENVOORDE AREA to camp at RENINGHELST. No. 3 Coy move to GANSPETTE with 123rd Infy Bde. General routine	
	7/4/17		General Routine.	
	8/4/17		General Routine. One H.Q. Horse on charge No. 1 Coy. died struck off.	
	9/4/17		General Routine	

41ST DIVISIONAL TRAIN ORDERLY ROOM

Army Form C. 2118

WAR DIARY
or
INTELLIGENCE SUMMARY
(Erase heading not required.)

Instructions regarding War Diaries and Intelligence Summaries are contained in F. S. Regs, Part II. and the Staff Manual respectively. Title Pages will be prepared in manuscript.

Place	Date	Hour	Summary of Events and Information	Remarks and references to Appendices
RENINGHELST Sheet 28 G 34 d Central	10/7/17		General Routine. Lieut H.D. Moses on charge No. 1 Coy. Arrested struck off. Capt. Y.R. Pennell No. 1 Coy returned to duty. Taken off sick list.	[sig]
	11/7/17		General Routine.	[sig]
	12/7/17		8 O.R.'s awarded 1st G.C. Badge. General Routine.	[sig]
	13/7/17		General Routine.	[sig]
	14/7/17		C.O. visits No 3 Coy in Training Area. Capt. J.J. Reynolds R.A.M.C. join vice Capt. Roy. Spencer, R.A.M.C. transferred. Lt. Stewart, A.C. No. T4/22791 No 2 Coy. transferred struck off from strength.	[sig]
	15/7/17		General Routine.	[sig]
	16/7/17		No. T4/22791 Dr. STEWART A.C. No. 2 Coy. rejoined from 2nd Canadian C.C.S. Taken on strength General Routine	[sig]
	17/7/17		4 H.D. Horses received from Remounts. Taken on strength posted to No. 1 Coy. Normal routine	[sig]
	18/7/17		No. T4/99738 Dr. Sdr K13326 WW. No. 1 Coy transferred to Base Depot, England to G.H.Q. struck off.	[sig]

WAR DIARY
INTELLIGENCE SUMMARY
(Erase heading not required.)

Army Form C. 2118

Place	Date	Hour	Summary of Events and Information	Remarks and references to Appendices
RENINGHELST Sheet 28 G.3.H.d. Central	19/7/17		Supply debit return to their Companies. 2nd/Lieut C.F. LOCHNER transferred from No. 4 to No. 2 (Company Train). General routine.	[sig]
	20/7/17		Refilling of supplies commenced at 10 a.m. No. T/026982 A/Cpl I'ANSON, C.F. No. 2 Coy, & No. T/060721 A/Cpl SCOTT S.D. No. 4 Coy, reverted to permanent grade of Driver, leaving surplus to establishment. General routine.	[sig]
	21/7/17		No. T/17266 S/Sadd. Sgt. STURGESS A.C. joined from 3rd Auxiliary Horse Trans. taken on strength. Two Dris Farriers from Base Depot (F.T.S.) from Base Remount at Office of 4 Coy to summer clothing. Presided, Cpl MORRIS A.S.C. Member: LT. C. TRIPP A.S.C. & 2/LT. G. WARRINGTON A.S.C. No. T/17266 S/Sadd/Sgt. STURGESS A.C. appointed S/Sch. S.Sgt. with pay. General routine.	[sig]
	22/7/17		No. T/M 172944 Pte DUNFORD C.R. No. 4 Coy. transferred to Rail Hd. Qrs. 2nd Army Irish Off. No. T/36497 Dr Hadley B. No. 2 Coy transferred to 136 H.T. Coy. Amb. strength of No. T/364452 Dr CARTWRIGHT T. No. 4 Coy. to 140 H.T. Amb. strength of Board of Officers assemble at office of 2 Coy to summer clothing. Presided, Cpl. A.S. LAPP. A.S.C. Member: LT. C. TRIPP. A.S.C. & 2/LT. G. WARRINGTON A.S.C.	[sig]
	23/7/17		No. T/33504 Dr COLGAN J. deserts from Base Detail, reported from Havelian at DUBLIN 28/7/17. General routine.	[sig]
	24/7/17		General routine	[sig]

WAR DIARY
or
INTELLIGENCE SUMMARY
(Erase heading not required.)

Army Form C. 2118

Place	Date	Hour	Summary of Events and Information	Remarks and references to Appendices
RENINGHELST Sheet 28 G 24 d Central	25/7/17		No. 3 Coy Train return to Camp at RENINGHELST from "Back Area". No. 2 Coy Train proceeds with 122 I Bde to Lederring Area. General Routine.	
	26/7/17		No. T/2/094239 Dr LOVALL G. No. 1 Coy evacuated 22/7 struck off. T/4/091843 Dr BAILEY F. No. 3 Coy evacuated 12/7 struck off. T/2/065293 Dr ROSIER A. No. 4 Coy, wounded by shrapnel for anti-aircraft shell – 23/7, evacuated 24/7 struck off. S4/043918 Cpl JOHNSTON E. No. 3 Coy attached to Divisional Headquarters for duty in E. Officers from this date. T/2/023782 Dr TATE T. No. 1 Coy discharged from Divt. Detention Camp this day. General routine.	
	27/7/17		General routine	
	28/7/17		No. T.2/11076 Dr LAWLOR P. No. 1 Coy admitted to Divt. Detention Camp. General routine. 5 H.D. Horses received from Remounts. Taken on strength.	
	29/7/17		One H.D. Horse No. 132 in charge No. 1 Coy died struck off. General routine.	
	30/7/17		No. T/2/213869 Dr Dodd Walter a journal from Base Depot 29th incl. taken on strength. General routine.	

1875 W. W393/826 1,000,000 4/15 – J.B.C. & A. – A.D.S.S./Forms/C.2118.

Army Form C. 2118

WAR DIARY
or
INTELLIGENCE SUMMARY
(Erase heading not required.)

Vol / 3

41st DIVISIONAL TRAIN — ORDERLY ROOM

Place	Date	Hour	Summary of Events and Information	Remarks and references to Appendices
RENINGHELST Shet 28 G.3.d Central	1/5/17		Lieut WTS MAILE A.S.C. slightly wounded, whilst inspecting Reserve Ration Dumps in Kinota, on 30/4/17. T/4/505293 Pte ROSIER A. No 4 Coy. rets to duty from 2 C.C.S. taken on strength. General Routine	[sig]
	2/5/17		General Routine	[sig]
	3/5/17		No T/4/251786 S.Sgt IRVING A (joined from 50th Divisional Train. posted to 3 Coy for C.S.M. (W.O. Class 2). Court of Enquiry assembled @ office of No. 3 Coy. Board of officers. General Routine	[sig]
	4/5/17		Court of Enquiry assembled at office of No. 3 Coy re inquiry to No. 9/11597 Pte Freeman G. 2/3 Middlesex Regt. attached 3 Coy Train. Presided Capt Fleming A.S.C. Lieut Br Pagh 2/Lieut EMc Zyll	[sig]
			General Routine.	
	5/5/17		No T/2/17076 Dr LAWLOR P. No 1 Coy returned from Park Detention Camp. No T/36538 Dr WILSON G. from No 1 Coy to Train H.Qrs. On officers charge. from 1 Coy to Broxo H.Q	[sig]
	6/5/17		No 54/065125 S.Sgt TAYLOR W.P. Train H.Qrs. appointed A/S.Q.M.S. from 25/4/17. 10 O.R. proceed to 2nd Army Rest Camps. AMBLETEUSE. General Routine.	[sig]

WAR DIARY
INTELLIGENCE SUMMARY
(Erase heading not required.)

Army Form C. 2118

Place	Date	Hour	Summary of Events and Information	Remarks and references to Appendices
RENINGHELST Sheet 28 G 34 d Central	7/5/17		F.G.C.M. of No. T/S/8125 Pte WEST G.E. No 3 Cy. Capt. POLLARD URQUHART A.S.C. presents. General Routine.	[signature]
	8/5/17		General Routine. No. T/4/094229 Pte LOVALL C. No 1 Cy rejoined from No 10 C.C.S. taken on strength.	[signature]
	9/5/17		F.G.C.M. on No. T/S/8125 Pte WEST G.E. formalised Charge "Drunkenness" Accused was found guilty sentenced to undergo 28 days F.P. No 2. General routine.	[signature]
	10/5/17		No T/4/069987 A/Sgt. JONES H. No 1 Cy transferred to A.S.C. Base depot to Duplex establishment. (Struck off) General routine.	[signature]
	11/5/17		On 9/S.S.M + 5 9/Sgts. attached 137, 139 & 140 Fd Ambs confirmed in rank. Authority A.S.C. Ro/3728. General Routine.	[signature]
	12/5/17		No 1 Coy move from 9.22 d.7.8.1 to M8c.3.8. No T/4/21380 S.S.M. Dudley L.A. A.S.C. to be 9/R.S.M. Vice No T/15003 S.S.M. Perry A.R. A.S.C. General routine. Due No 9 Horse in charge No 1 Coy destroyed. Struck off.	[signature]
	13/5/17		16 Fm of Train H.Q. & No. 1 Coy awarded 1st G.C. Badge. General routine.	[signature]
	14/5/17		5 Men of No. 2.3 & 4 Coys awarded 1st G.C. Badge.	[signature]

Army Form C. 2118

WAR DIARY
INTELLIGENCE SUMMARY
(Erase heading not required.)

Place	Date	Hour	Summary of Events and Information	Remarks and references to Appendices
RENINGHELST Sheet 28 G.2.d. Central	15/5/17		J.G.6.7y of No. I 335504 D COLGAN J. No. 1 Company. Capt J.S WHEATER A.S.C. proceeded 5 Days transferred to 189th Bde RFA (A.F.A.) from No. 1 Cy. 5 Days " " from —— to —— to No. 1 Cy. 4 Reinforcement join from Base Depot. Taken on Strength. General Routine	
	16/5/17		General Routine. Two N.D. husars in charge No 2 Cy presented struck off.	
	17/5/17		General Routine. No. 4 Cy went with 124th D.Bde to Back Area	
	18/5/17		21. PULLEINE A.S.C proceeded to No 5 BASE Remount Depot to 100 O/R's for 200 Remounts for Division. General Routine	
	19/5/17		Capt the Rev L.W BROWN. C.F. joined 14th Divnl. attached to No 1 Cy. General Routine	
	20/5/17		No 744 25 786 S/Sgt IRVING A. No. 3 Cy Promoted C.S.M. (W.O. cl 2) with effect from 4 Current authority A.S.E Section, Base. No. A.S.C. P.M./1553/109 of 14/5/17 General Routine	
	21/5/17		General Routine	

WAR DIARY

INTELLIGENCE SUMMARY

(Erase heading not required.)

Army Form C. 2118

Place	Date	Hour	Summary of Events and Information	Remarks and references to Appendices
RENINGHELST Sheet 28 G 34 d Central.	22/5/17		F.G.C.M. of No. T/33504 D' Colgan J. promulgated. Charges:- (1). Desertion (2). Loss of kit. Found guilty on both charges. Sentence Bandago 90 days F.P. No 1. Report for entries of kit Cool. 1 No. T3/026912 D' I'Anson C.F. No. 2 Coy. & No. T/660921 D' Scott S.J. No. 4 Coy reinstated in the appointment of A/Corporal from 20th April 1917 inclusive. Authority A.S.C. Section. Base No. 8/621.3/5 of 4 May 17. 200 Remounts arrived by road from No. 5 Remount Depot. CALAIS & are distributed to Units of Division on strength prior to No. 1 Coy. 2 H.D. Lines received from Remounts taken on strength prior. General Routine	[signature]
	23/5/17		No T/33504 D' Colgan J. No. 1 Coy admitted into Div. Detention Camp. General Routine.	[signature]
	24/5/17		No T/4/065233 D' Cole F. No. 1 Company admitted into Div. Detention Camp. General routine.	[signature]
	25/5/17		T/Capt. V.H. Pennell A.S.C. found medically fit for General Service. Struck off strength from 12th inst. No. S/307415 Pte Dunn D.B. joined from Base Depot. General routine.	[signature]

WAR DIARY or INTELLIGENCE SUMMARY

Army Form C. 2118

(Erase heading not required.)

Place	Date	Hour	Summary of Events and Information	Remarks and references to Appendices
RENINGHELST Sheet 28 d 6.34 d Central	26/5/17		No. T3/026982 A/Cpl. I'ANSON. C.F. No. 2 Cy. No. T4/066721 A/Cpl. SCOTT. S.D. No. 4 Cy. Ceased to be attached, proceeded to Base Depot, HAVRE. Struck off General routine	[signature]
	27/5/17		Lieut. C. TRIPP A.S.C. returned to duty. Taken off sick list. H. 49 horses received from Remount, taken on strength. 4. H.9 horses + on Riding horse wounded by shell fire in forward area. General routine	[signature]
	28/5/17		No. T2/112241 Corpl. HASTINGS. D. No. 4 Cy. killed by shell fire in forward area struck off strength. No. T/32532 A/Sergt HINES. J. No. 1 Cy. wounded by shell fire No. T4/0944275 Pte. MILBURN. D. No. 2 Cy. wounded by shell fire - admitted 58th Fd Amby. struck off. No. T/365448 Pte. MINSHULL. J. No. 3 Cy. wounded by shell fire - admitted No. 2. C.C.C.S. struck off. One riding horse in charge No. 4 Cy. destroyed by shell fire - struck off One H.9 horse in charge No. 2 Cy. wounded by shell fire. No. T4/066721 Dr THORPE. A. No. 1 Cy. evacuated to Base from No. 15th C.C.S. n 1573/17 struck off.	[signature]

Army Form C. 2118

WAR DIARY
INTELLIGENCE SUMMARY
(Erase heading not required.)

Place	Date	Hour	Summary of Events and Information	Remarks and references to Appendices
RENINGHELST Sheet 28 G.3 + d Central	29/5/17		The remains of the late Corpl HASTINGS J. buried in VLAMERTINGHE MILITARY CEMETERY Sheet 28. H.3.c.2.2. Grave No. 14 Row 'A'. No. T/094275 Dr MILBURN.D. No. 2 Coy died of wounds in No. 2.C.C.S. General routine.	
	30/5/17		The remains of the late Dr MILBURN D. buried in BAILLEUL MILITARY CEMETERY. T/ied R. HARRIS A.S.C. joined from Base Depot. Taken on strength. General Routine.	
	31/5/17		78 O/Rs 1cn from 405 Labour Coy (5th Divl. Employmt Coy) in relief of London etc taken on strength + posted as follows. Westgarth-Lain No. 1 Coy — 6 " 2 " — 30 " 3 " — 16 " 4 " — 12 — 14 General routine. Railhead OUDERDOM for 3 Canal material. No. T/3/R 03774 Dr STEELE C.J. + No. TS8228 Dr GRANT A.E. No. 1 Coy. arrested (Gassed). struck off. Approximate detail nightly working for C.R.E. in forward area 40 90/10.	

Army Form C. 2118.

WAR DIARY
or
INTELLIGENCE SUMMARY
(Erase heading not required.)

Instructions regarding War Diaries and Intelligence Summaries are contained in F. S. Regs., Part II. and the Staff Manual respectively. Title Pages will be prepared in manuscript.

Place	Date	Hour	Summary of Events and Information	Remarks and references to Appendices
RENINGHELST Shut 28 G.3 and Central	1/6/17		On riding line a Large 3 Cy destroyed 29 Bulls. struck off. General Routine.	*sig*
	2/6/17		2. N.C.O's on a charge No.1 Cy killed by shell fire — struck off. No T/28228 D/Gaul E. No.1 Cy Returned to Duty from 138th Fld Amb. General routine.	*sig*
	3/6/17		General routine.	*sig*
	4/6/17		1 Mule a Large No.3 Cy evacuated to No. 23 Veterinary H. 31 Bulls — struck off. No SY/07011 Cpl NAISMITH A.N. appointed N/Sergt No SY/042323 L/Cpl RICHARDSON M. appointed L/Cpl.	*sig*
	5/6/17		General routine. No.T/457 N° 0574437 A/S CHURCHILL.W.A.M. No.4 Cy evacuated to C.C.S. 4 Lines. Gassed (shell) — struck off. T/Lieut N.T.S. MAILE to be T/Captain. Extract from London Gazette 4/9/17. Extract from London Gazette 4/9/17. Awarded the "Distinguished Service Order" Lieut Colonel W.W.Molony N.S.C.	*sig*
	6/6/17		Extract from London Gazette 29th May 1917. Mentioned in Despatch Lieut. Col. W.W. MOLONY A.S.C. D.D. GALBRAITH L.S. LAPP Captain	

WAR DIARY
or
INTELLIGENCE SUMMARY

(Erase heading not required.)

Army Form C. 2118.

Place	Date	Hour	Summary of Events and Information	Remarks and references to Appendices
RENINGHELST Sheet 28 J.34.d Central	6/7/17	cont	One riding horse transferred from No. 1 Coy to No. 3 Coy.	[sig]
	7/6/17		General routine. One Riding Horse in charge of No. 3 Coy destroyed. H.Q. - Cast of.	[sig]
	8/6/17		T/Captain B.W. PARKE R.A.S.C. to be T/Major. Subject to promulgation T/Lieut. C. TRIPP. A.S.C. to be T/Captain in London Gazette. General routine.	[sig]
	9/6/17		2 H.Q. horses in charge No. 2 & 3 Coys evacuated - attack of. General routine.	[sig]
	10/6/17		W.O. S/07016 S/Sgt WAISMITH A.M No. 2 Coy placed on 5'-Wreck Corps pay from 28/4/17. 5 H.Q. horses + 1 mule procured for Remount, status in charge. One H.Q. horse in charge No. 4 remounted of Cist. attack of. General routine.	[sig]
	11/6/17		General routine.	[sig]
	12/6/17		One mule transferred from No. 2 to No. 3 Coy. Two H.Q. Horse in charge of No. 4 Coy remounted 272116. Church off No. 044402 a/s. Sgt. JENKINS W.P. 1/6 L Coy confined in ready of Staff Sgt Curatory. A.S.C. M074. 2/9/17	[sig]

Army Form C. 2118.

WAR DIARY
or
INTELLIGENCE SUMMARY
(Erase heading not required.)

Instructions regarding War Diaries and Intelligence Summaries are contained in F.S. Regs., Part II. and the Staff Manual respectively. Title Pages will be prepared in manuscript.

Place	Date	Hour	Summary of Events and Information	Remarks and references to Appendices
RENINGHELST Sheet 28 G. 31 d Central	12/9/17	(cont)	No.T/325332 L/Cpl. (a/Sgt.) HINES. J. No.1 Cy Promoted Corpl. 5/3/17. Authority A.S.C. Order No.14.9.1917. General routine. De MO. Hure No. 140 recruits - struck of	
	13/9/17		Move of Companies from Nos.1,3 to G.36 a.6. & Nos.2,4 to G.36 a.3.7 Sheet 28. General routine. No.1 Cy died - struck of On H.Q. Horse in charge No.1 Cy	
	14/9/17		No.T/36851 D. COLLIER H. No. 4 Cy admitted into Divl. Detention Camp. General routine	
	15/9/17		T/3/0237415 D. YOXALL A. No.2 Cy Deserted - struck of 12 Sept. General routine.	
	16/9/17		General routine. No.T/SR.02471 Dr Oxley J. No.1 Cy to No.4 Cy No.T/36538 Driver H. No.4 Cy to No.1 Cy	
	17/9/17		General routine Railhead moved from OUDERDOM to WIPPENHOEK	
	18/9/17		SW/070722 Cpl. Satterthwaite D. No. 3 Cy appointed a/Sgt. Authority a/s.c. SW/070721 Pte Gray L. No.4 Cy appointed a/Cpl. P.12/4819/15 SW/070722 a/Sgt Satterthwaite from No.3 Cy to From Miller. SW/99971 Pte Grey from 4 Cy to No.3 Cy. No.S/307415 Platoon T. Hobbs Pillow Cy.	

Army Form C. 2118.

WAR DIARY
or
INTELLIGENCE SUMMARY
(Erase heading not required.)

Instructions regarding War Diaries and Intelligence Summaries are contained in F. S. Regs., Part II. and the Staff Manual respectively. Title Pages will be prepared in manuscript.

Place	Date	Hour	Summary of Events and Information	Remarks and references to Appendices
RENINGHELST Sheet 28 E.3.d central	19/9/17		4 Reinforcements Men from Base Depot. Lakes in Ctg.M. 18 men W.E.F. 2404 373. L/Cpl Evans M. No 1 Cy to No. 3 Cy. General routine	[initials]
	20/9/17		21 O/Rank arrested 1st F.C. Bnde. No. 2465233 Dmr. Cole. F. No. 1 Cy released from Ord. Detn. Comp. General routine	[initials]
	21/9/17		All Coys return to RENINGHEST. Captain S. Culllurd 2 Cy placed on List Zer. General routine	[initials]
	22/9/17		Coys move to Sheet 28. M.3.6.6.6. Hute Camp. General routine	[initials]
	23/9/17		Coys move to Sheet 28. M.14 central. Hute camps. General routine	[initials]
	24/9/17		No. T.W 035913 D Fm. PHILLIPS, F.J. No. 2 Cy \ Returned to Base Depot 21 Divl. No. 73/027471 D Fm. TIMBERLAKE, W. No.4 Cy / Surplus to established. Struck off General routine.	[initials]
	25/9/17		General Routine.	[initials]
	26/9/17		General Routine. Reinforcement from WIPPENHOEK to RENINGHELST.	[initials]

WAR DIARY
INTELLIGENCE SUMMARY
(Erase heading not required.)

Army Form C. 2118

Instructions regarding War Diaries and Intelligence Summaries are contained in F.S. Regs., Part II. and the Staff Manual respectively. Title Pages will be prepared in manuscript.

Place	Date	Hour	Summary of Events and Information	Remarks and references to Appendices
RENINGHELST Sheet 26 M. + a.6.8.	27/7/17		Capt. D.G. GALBRAITH, invalided to England from N° 1st General P. 26th. Struck off Lieut Joseph Stella assumes temporary command of N° 2 Cy N° 7/15737 D/ MANLEY P.A. N° 3 Cy granted one month leave (28/7/17 - 27/8/17) General routine.	
	28/7/17		N° 2 Cy move to Red area Sheet 27. R.32.d.9.5. 2 Reinforcements join for three Depots. Taken on Strength On R.O. Have a charge N° 3 Cy November — struck off General routine.	
	29/7/17		General reporting. Transfer. 2/L CMCLUFF. Not attd to N° 2 Cy. 2/L C.FLOCHNER. N° 2 Cy to Hd Qr Trans	
	30/7/17		N° 4 Cy move to Sheet 27. X + a.8.7. General routine	

J.B. Rewton
Corpl / Adjt for
Commanding H/Qr Div Train

WAR DIARY
or
INTELLIGENCE SUMMARY

(Erase heading not required.)

Army Form

Instructions regarding War Diaries and Intelligence Summaries are contained in F.S. Regs, Part II. and the Staff Manual respectively. Title Pages will be prepared in manuscript.

Place	Date	Hour	Summary of Events and Information	Remarks and references to Appendices
METEREN Sheet 27 X.15.d.7.5	1/7/16		Gram Hd Ofrs move to METEREN No 3 Cy move to THIEDSHOUK AREA. Q.3.W.d.8.4. General routing. Railhead CAESTRE from 30th Ulto.	MP
	2/7/17		On HQ move in charge No.1 Cy recruited 27 ORs struck off & Reinforcements from Base Depot Jake in charge.	MP
	3/7/17		General routine.	MP
	4/7/17		General routine. 3. HQ Lorries received from Remount Depot - CALAIS.	MP
	5/7/17		The undermentioned recruited in late n strated struck off strength. T/4 DC5233 D Coles F. No.1. Cy - 28/6/17 T/ER 03744 D Rudge A. No.2. - 27/6/17 T/11334 D Elmslie G No.4 - 23/6/17	MP
	6/7/17		On HQ Lorie No 29, in charge No.1 Cy. admitted 2nd London Fd Vet Section, for evacuation. 5 ORs struck off. No.1 Cy move to SCHAEXKEN	MP
	7/7/17		On HQ Lorie in charge No 2 Cy. died - struck off strength. T/108310 Cpl. Middleditch H. No.1 Cy recruited 28 ORs - struck off	MP

WAR DIARY
or
INTELLIGENCE SUMMARY

Army Form C. 2118.

Place	Date	Hour	Summary of Events and Information	Remarks and references to Appendices
MEEREN Sheet 27 X.15.d.7.5	8/7/17		Bn H.Q. have in charge No. 2 Coy admitted 52709 N.V. Section for execution 5th Lieut of No. T/044953. 2 Lt. SMITH J. No. 3 Coy rejoined 2nd Lieut of our strick of	M.P.
	9/7/17		T/2568 Sgt. PHILLIPS. A. No. S/044953 of No. 1 Coy proceeded to England to take up temporary commission — Struck off strength of No. 1 Coy. No. S/04-2323 A/Cpl RICHARDSON M. No. 1 Coy reverted to P. grade of L/Cpl.	M.P.
	10/7/17		T/Capt. E.M. WOOD joined from 5th Cavalry Divn A.S.C. Taken on strength speed No. T/36851 2Lt COLLIER H. 4 Coy completed centers of 2 Coy F.P.I. to No 2 Coy.	M.P.
	11/7/17		No. 3 Coy. Operate 12 hour	M.P.
	12/7/17		Normal routine	M.P.
	13/7/17		No. 4 Coy Operate Lieut R. HARRIS proceeded to ABBEVILLE for course of instruction in transport duties	M.P.
	14/7/17		Normal routine	M.P.
	15/7/17		Capt/Adjt J.B. WHEATER M.C., A.S.C. proceeded to O.T.H.Q for attachment. Lieut M. POOLEY assumes the duties of A/Adjutant from 16 hour.	M.P.

WAR DIARY or INTELLIGENCE SUMMARY

Army Form C. 2118.

Place	Date	Hour	Summary of Events and Information	Remarks and references to Appendices
METEREN Sht 27 X 15 d 7.5	16/7/17		Sir Sfranks inspected 1st G.L. Bridge. Divisional Commander inspected No. 3 rt Coy.	M.P.
	17/7/17		Divisional Commander inspected No. 1 & 2 Coy. One H.Q. Lorie No. 93 in charge No. 3 Coy destroyed by enett. (struck off)	M.P.
	18/7/17		No. 4 Coy moved to HEKSKEN Sht 28 M.3.C.1.2. No. T4/026235 Corpl EVERATT J. No. 2 Coy invalided to 3rd Canadian C.C.S. on 14th inst. (struck off)	M.P.
	19/7/17		No. T/294249 Dr MORRISON D.S., 2 H.Q Lorries + 1 G.S. wagon join from 238th M.G. Coy. No. T4/65-7681 Dr OXBERRY J. No. 4 Coy deposed 3 days pay forfeit. G.C. Hodge.	M.P.
	20/7/17		L. 13.6. M. ANDREW No. 3 Coy & No. 4 Coy. T4/213869 Dr Saddl/ WALKER, T.H.Q to No. 4 Coy.	M.P.
	21/7/17		No. T4/057482 Dr STOTT. No. 4 Coy invalided to C.C.S. 16 Cines struck off. One H.Q Lorie in charge No. 2 Coy + 1 Mule in charge No. 1 Coy invalided 19 Cines. (struck off) 4 Reinforcement joint from Arm Depot 12km in strength No. 3 Coy move to M10. B.6.5.	M.P.

WAR DIARY
or
INTELLIGENCE SUMMARY

(Erase heading not required.)

Army Form C. 2118.

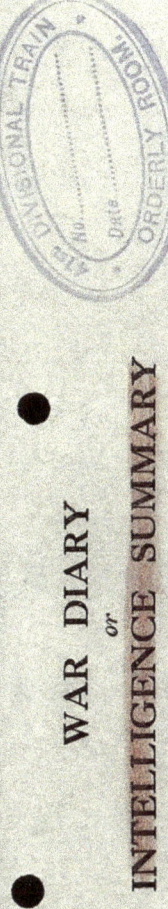

Place	Date	Hour	Summary of Events and Information	Remarks and references to Appendices
METEREN Sht 27 x.15.d.7.5.	22/7/17		T/36565 D/ Dean A.H. No. 2 Cy evacuated to 15 C.C.S. 12 Lines. Attack of our Ridn were H.B. Line in charge No. 3 Cy. evacuated 19th attack of.	MP
	23/7/17		Lieut Colonel W.W. Molony, D.S.O. A.S.C. Officer commanding, admitted (sick) into 58th Stationary General Hospital. Major B.W. Parker assumes temporary command of the formation. Senior Hd Offr moves to BOESCHEPE Sheet 27. R.9. d.9.4.	MP
BOESCHEPE Sht 27 R.9.d.9.4.	24/7/17		Our mule in charge No.1 Cy evacuated 23 Lines. attack of.	MP
	25/7/17		Railhead changed from CAESTRE to BRULOOZE.	MP
WESTOUTRE Sht 28 M.15.a.6.8	26/7/17		Senior Hd Offr moved to WESTOUTRE - a/noon of 25th M.15. A.3.9. No.4 Cy moves to M.11. A.3.9.	MP
	27/7/17		No.T/4378 D/ Cullen P. No.1 Cy wounded by shrapnel 1 Rider killed & 3 H.D. Lines in charge No.1 Cy wounded by shrapnel Major P.W. Prockter A.S.C. assumes command of Train vice Major B.W. Parker	MP

WAR DIARY
or
INTELLIGENCE SUMMARY

(Erase heading not required.)

Army Form C. 2118.

Place	Date	Hour	Summary of Events and Information	Remarks and references to Appendices
WESTOUTRE Sheet 28 M.15.a.6.8.	28/7/17		No. 201485 Sgt ROSEN, 238" Emp. Cy joined. Robt 16 "3 Cy. No. T.3/624490 Dr GAVAN. J. No. 2 Cy evacuated to No. 11. C.C.S. on 24 inst struck off. 3. M.O. Lvce. Nos. 107, 108, 144 enlarge No. 1. Cy. wounded by Shrapnel on 27th and evacuated. struck off. 1. HQ hrse enlarge No. 4 Cy evacuation. struck off.	M.O. M.O. M.O.
	29/7/17		Manuel work	M.O.
	30/7/17		4. Reinforcements join from Base Depot taken on strength. No. T4/085310 Dr TURNBULL, R.H. No. 2 Cy. No. T4/057889 Dr ORR. D. No. 3 Cy + No. T4/065300 Dr HARRIS E transfered to 138th Fd Amb. struck off. Lieut A.L. M Andrew No. 4 Cy to No. 3 Cy. 2/Lieut. N. PULLEIN/E No. 3 Cy proceeded to England to undergo a course of instruction in Infantry Duties. Struck off. Lieut. Colonel W.W. MOLONY. D.S.O. A.S.C. evacuated to England from No. 5.8. General Base Hospital.	M.O.
	31/7/17		No. T/78737 Dr MANLEY. P.A. No. 3 Cy transferred to 7 Fd. Amb. 12.7.17 Adm. Struck off. No. T/35738 Dr WOODCOCK W.J. injured from H.Qtr. 12.7.17 J Adl. reported to No. 3 Cy.	M.O. to Coming. 41 & 20 Train.

Army Form C. 2118.

WAR DIARY
or
INTELLIGENCE SUMMARY
(Erase heading not required.)

Instructions regarding War Diaries and Intelligence Summaries are contained in F. S. Regs., Part II. and the Staff Manual respectively. Title Pages will be prepared in manuscript.

Place	Date	Hour	Summary of Events and Information	Remarks and references to Appendices
WESTOUTRE Sheet 28 M.15. a. 6.6.	1/9/17		No. T/5883 A/S.S.M. PERRY. A.R. to be A/R.S.M. vice T/213880 S.S.M. DUDLEY. L.A. No. T/4373 Dr CULLEN. P. No. 1 Coy transferred to No. 41. C.C.S. on 27th inst. Struck off	M.P.
	2/9/17		2/Lieut C.M.C. LUFF. No. 2 Coy to No. 1 Coy. No. T/18883 Sergt. (A/S.S.M.) PERRY. A.R. promoted C.Q.M.S. with effect from 5-9-17. Authority A.S.C. Order No.78/1917.	M.P.
	3/9/17		Dr. A.O. LOVE No. 33 i/c large No. 2 Coy killed by shrapnel. Struck off S. A.O. received from Remounts. Taken on strength.	M.P.
	4/9/17		Nine Driver (reinforcements) received from Base Depot. Taken on strength. No. T/4 233814 Driver WIGGINS. G.W. No. 1 Coy. killed by shell fire this day. LA CLYTTE Sheet 28 N 7 c 8.9. Buried 5th Army Military Cemetery.	M.P.
	5/9/17		No. T/36753 Dr FINCH G.W. No. 2 Coy deprived of G.C. Badge. 28th inst.	M.P.
	6/9/17		Five reinforcements received from Remount Base Depot. Taken on strength. 3 Rider transferred to 2nd Army Remount Section Under authority A.G.S. G.H.Q. No. O/B/2038 of 1/9/17 - 11 Riding Horse become Complete re-establishment. Re-designated by D.D.V.S. as L.S.	M.P.

WAR DIARY or INTELLIGENCE SUMMARY

Army Form C. 2118.

Place	Date	Hour	Summary of Events and Information	Remarks and references to Appendices
WESTOUTRE Sheet 28 N 15. a. 6.8.	6/8/17	Cont.	Rackham today visited troops notice BAILLEUL No. T/592526 Pte NUNN. N. No. 3 Coy to Fd. Off. 123rd Fd Bde struck off No. T/335204 Pte COLGAN J. No. 1 Coy admitted to No. 87 C.C.S. on train struck off	M.O.
	7/8/17		Nowt yookie.	M.O.
	8/8/17		No. T3/027002 Sgt HAMILTON A. No. 1 Coy wounded by shell fire struck off One H.D. Horse wounded by shell fire. One HD Horse No. 93 on large No. 26 wounded. struck off	M.O.
	9/8/17		Captain L.S. LADD. A.S.C. posted to R.F.C. struck off Captain J.J. REYNOLDS R.A.M.C. M/O to Train posted to 139th Fd Amb One Rider No. 13 on large No. 2 Coy Evacuated on a Draught Horse, posted to No. 2 Coy. struck off	M.O.
	10/8/17		Capt. J.J. REYNOLDS. R.A.M.C. temporarily attached as M/O to Train T/SR 01713 Pte WINTON J.E. No. 1 Coy Evacuated 24/7/17 T/M/24412 Pte BARTLETT J. No. 4 " " 3/8/17 struck off T3/027002 Sgt HAMILTON No. 1 " " 8/8/17	M.I.

WAR DIARY or INTELLIGENCE SUMMARY

Army Form C. 2118.

Place	Date	Hour	Summary of Events and Information	Remarks and references to Appendices
WESTOUTRE Sheet 28 N.15.a.6.8.	11/8/17		No. S/290520 Pte PRINOLD F.H. 2nd Hd Qts to No. 1 Coy from 12th Fnd. Railhead BRULOOZE from today. On Hd Qrs. have in charge No. 1 Coy died of wounds. Struck off	M.P.
	12/8/17		Major T. DOWLING A.S.C. (T.F.) joined from 3rd Divl. Train taken on strength. S/No. 065:25. C/S.D.M.S.y. confirmed in rank of A.D.M.S. Authority A.L.C. No. 20192 d/11/8/17. No. 3 Coy awarded 12 Q.B. Badges 5 Officers mine to FOUNTAINE HOUCK + A.B.6	M.P.
	13/8/17		Major T. DOWLING A.S.C. appointed A/Lt. Colonel from this date inclusive Lieut Col. T. DOWLING assume command of this formation. Lieut Col. W.W. MOLONY D.S.O. A.S.C. invalided to England from date Struck off T/Lieut G.W. GREY, T/2 Lt J.B. ASTON + T/2 Lt S. COOKSON posted from Base Captain E.M. RUTTER A.S.C. Train H.Qrs. appointing D.A.Q.M.G. 2nd Army Struck off strength from 12th inst	M.P.
	14/8/17		No. 2 Coy move to R.19.d.5.7.	M.P.
	15/8/17		Train Hd Qrs move to METEREN Sheet 27 x.15.d.7.5. No. 4 Coy move to Q.29.d.8.7.	M.P.

WAR DIARY
or
INTELLIGENCE SUMMARY

(Erase heading not required.)

Army Form C. 2118.

Place	Date	Hour	Summary of Events and Information	Remarks and references to Appendices
METEREN Sheet 27 X.15.d.7.5	16/8/17		Seven H.Q. horses received from Remounts. Taken on strength.	M.P.
	17/8/17		No. T/058109 Dr Butcher W.H. No. 4 Cy evacuated to C.C.S. 14th knocked off	M.P.
	18/8/17		2nd Lieut. G. Warrington A.S.C. killed & 2nd Lieut. S. Cookson A.S.C. wounded by a bomb dropped by enemy aircraft.	M.P.
	19/8/17		No. T/35751 Dr Appleber H.T.W. No. 3 Cy to H.d. Qts. 123 Inf. Bde. struck off. No. T/36898 Dr Collins G.C. from H.d. Qts. 123 Inf. Bde. Taken on strength. Remains of late 2/Lt G. Warrington A.S.C. Buried Mep. reference sheet 27 S.E. Q.29.d.59.	M.P.
	20/8/17		No. T/13373 Dr Jordan J.W. No. 4 Cy evacuated to 11th C.C.S. n. 15th Inst. Struck off. No. 2 Cy move to Acquin sheet 27A S.E. V.16.a.5.0 No. 3 Cy move to Esquerdes sheet 36D. N.E. E5.c.6.0. 7.G.C.M. of No. T/065293 Dr Rosier A. No. 4 Cy 19 Inst.	M.P.
	21/8/17		Train Hd. Qts. move to Wizernes sheet 36D. N.E. F.2 d. P.2.	M.P.
WIZERNES Sheet 36d. NE F.2 d.8.2	22/8/17		Moved rations. Ration drawn from Detail Issue Stor at St Omer.	M.P.

WAR DIARY
or
INTELLIGENCE SUMMARY.
(Erase heading not required.)

Army Form C. 2118.

Place	Date	Hour	Summary of Events and Information	Remarks and references to Appendices
WIZERNES Sheet 26D.NE F.2.d.8.2	23/7/17		No. T/4/244375 A/Cpl. Evans awarded 1st G.C. Badge fm 5/8/16	M.P
	24/7/17		The undermentioned A/S.S.M. promoted temporary W.O. class 1 for duration of war. with effect from 2nd May 1917.  T/15863 A/S.S.M. PERRY A.R. T/13119 A/S.S.M EYCOTT F. T/14568 A/S.S.M DUGGAN H.T. Authority A.S.C. Records Wound No. CR/2969A/A/128 + A.S.C./Actn. No. P13/5769	M.P
	25/7/17		Usual routine	M.P
	26/7/17		One 140 Lorry No. 109 on charge No.1 Coy. Cast on 28th July 1917 – Struck off Authority 2nd Army No. Q/26809/2 of 22/8/17 + A.2 Division No. 8/17/72 of 24/7/17	M.P
	27/7/17		No.T/4/057M35 Dvr. Dall. M. No. 3 Coy to Art Ohs 123rd. Att via No. 293526 Dr. Murran.M returned to No.3 Coy. 18/7/17 C.O. inspects 1st Line Transport of 1.2.3.rd Coys. 18/7/17 D. Note	M.P
	28/7/17		Six reinforcements joined from Horse Depôt. Take a strength. No.T/4/173499 Pte. DONFORD C.R. approved from H.Q. Ohs 2nd Army 27/7/inst T/2nd J.S. STEWARD A.S.C. joined from Horse Depôt. On proceeding Embarkment to No. 236 M.T. Coy	M.P

WAR DIARY
or
INTELLIGENCE SUMMARY.
(Erase heading not required.)

Army Form C. 2118.

Place	Date	Hour	Summary of Events and Information	Remarks and references to Appendices
WIZERNES Sheet 36D NE	29/9/17		M.T. Mgmt Pte GUNFORD C.B. sick to Base. Quartermaster Instituted one H.Q. horse No. 126 on Lines No. 1 Coy detached	M.P.
F.2.d.2.2.	30/9/17		Mount routine	M.P.
		3 P.M.	Mount routine	M.P.

M. Bates Lieut.
Comdg. 41st Div. Train A.S.C.

Army Form C. 2118.

WAR DIARY
or
INTELLIGENCE SUMMARY.
(Erase heading not required.)

Place	Date	Hour	Summary of Events and Information	Remarks and references to Appendices
WIZERNES Sheet 36.q.NE F.2.d.8.2	1/9/17		Cpl. A.L. Woodcock 11th R W Kent Regt. joined 31st Batt. for course of instruction in Lewis Gunnery. From H.Q. Lewis. No. 46, 65, 90, 183 in charge No. 4 Coy. & 1, 149, 160, 80 in charge No. 1 Coy. Transmitted – Struck off.	CSM
	2/9/17		No. 1 Coy came to Sheet 27 S.E. R.3.c.7.4.	CSM
	3/9/17		E.O. inspected 1st Line Transport of 1.2 & 2 Bns. Horses ridden.	CSM
	4/9/17		F.G.C.M. of No. T2/SR.01405 C.S.M. WIGSTON T. No. 4 Coy. Charge (1) Drunkenness. 2. Conduct to the Prejudice of good order & Military discipline. Sleeping in the Forge after 9 P.M. Cted. 3. Striking a sentinel after 9 P.M.	CSM
	5/9/17		No. T2/SR.01405 C.S.M. WIGSTON T. No. 4 Coy. found NOT GUILTY of above charges. No. R/10947 Rfn. ADAMS A. 18th K.R.R.C. having completed a course of instruction in cold shoeing is to remain	CSM
	6/9/17		No. T2/SR.01405 C.S.M. WIGSTON T. No. 4 Coy. to No. 3 Coy. No. T4/251786 C.S.M. IRVING A. No. 3 Coy. to No. 4 Coy.	CSM
	7/9/17		No. T/13938 Dvr BANNER N. No. 2 Coy 16/138th Fk Amby – Struck off. No. T4/057480 D. Shipton Ln No. 4 Coy transferred to C.C.S. & 31st Field. Struck off. One Officer Charge on Charge.	CSM

WAR DIARY
or
INTELLIGENCE SUMMARY.
(Erase heading not required.)

Army Form C. 2118.

Place	Date	Hour	Summary of Events and Information	Remarks and references to Appendices
WIZERNES Sheet 36 D NE F 2 d. 9. 2	8/9/17		No. T/292440 S/s PARRISH E. No. 3 Coy transferred to Mot Stationary P. on 5th inst. & s/s roped 1st Line Transport 122 Coy. Bde. 7th Army struck off	WSM
	9/9/17		7 Reinforcements joined from Base Depot.	WSM
	10/9/17		Major T. DOWNING A.S.C. (TF) to be Lieut Colonel with precedence June 1st 1916 (Sept 8/05) Extract from London Gazette 7/9/17. No. T4/041268 S/s NEWTON J. No. 1 Coy transferred to No. 11 C.C.S. 2 this month off	WSM
	11/9/17		6 Hands awarded 1st G.C. Badge. Six. H.D. Horses received from No. 23. Vet. P. taken on strength. One H.D. + 2 L.D. (mules) received from Remounts, taken on strength. T/321. E. MAIN A.S.C. joined from Base Depot, taken on strength.	WSM
	12/9/17		One H.D. Horse No. 112 in charge No. 1 Coy evacuated 12 mur. sick off	WSM
	13/9/17		No. T4/057450 S/s SHIPTON L.V. returned from C.C.S. taken on strength.	WSM
	14/9/17		No. 2. 3. + 4 Coys + Train H.Q. transferred move to WALLEN CAPPEL area One H.D. Horse No. 79 in charge No. 2 Coy. died struck off.	WSM

Army Form C. 2118.

WAR DIARY
or
INTELLIGENCE SUMMARY.
(Erase heading not required.)

Instructions regarding War Diaries and Intelligence Summaries are contained in F. S. Regs., Part II. and the Staff Manual, respectively. Title pages will be prepared in manuscript.

Place	Date	Hour	Summary of Events and Information	Remarks and references to Appendices
WIZERNES Sheet 36d NE	15/9/17		Orders Not Ak from to ZEVECOTEN Sheet 28 NW G 35 c 3.5	
F.2.d.6.2			No.2 Coy move from WALLEN CAPPEL AREA to LE ROUKLOSHILLE	WSM
			No.3 " " " " to METEREN	
			No.4 " " " " to THIEUSHOCK	WSM
ZEVECOTEN Sheet 28 NW G.35.c.3.5	16/9/17		Railhead OUDERDOM from today. Nos 2 & 4 Coy move to N1 a 8.7. No 3 Coy to M5 c 3.5	WSM
			No. 79431 Pte Newton S. No 1 Coy reprsnt from C.C.S. no 10 and	
			5 category B check from Base depot in relief of category A check	
	17/9/17		No. 45/3894 Pte Froggatt No.1 Co 6 C.C.S. 9 thereat Sickness Off	WSM
			No. 745/249 Pte Saunders W No 4 Co to C.C.S. 6 " "	
	18/9/17		On category "B" check rsmrt from Base depot in relief of a category A check	WSM
			Cpl J.S. Woodcock, 11th R.W. Kent. Regsmn his School having completed course in Int Observing	
	19/9/17		5 following category "A" checks transferred to Base depot. No S/04w293 Cpl Lay (Sig.) No S/04w395 Cpl (Sig.) S/033699 Pte Fenwick A.C. S/035699 Pte Greenhill A. S/055758 Pte Howard A. Hall G.F. S/06028 Pte Johnson W. S/06678704 Pte Ruskin G.H. S/067074	WSM

WAR DIARY
or
INTELLIGENCE SUMMARY.

(Erase heading not required.)

Army Form C. 2118.

Instructions regarding War Diaries and Intelligence Summaries are contained in F.S. Regs., Part II. and the Staff Manual respectively. Title pages will be prepared in manuscript.

Place	Date	Hour	Summary of Events and Information	Remarks and references to Appendices
ZEVECOTEN Sheet 28 NW G.35.c.3.5.	20/7/17		T/2nd/LSG ALDOUS, A.S.C. joined from Base Depot on 19th inst. No. T/14568 T/SSM DUGGAN, HJ assumes duties of A/RSM. Lt B.E.M. ANDREW, A.S.C. proceeded to Depôt Field Survey Coy for 1 month attachment or probation 19.7.	codm
	21/7/17		No. T/108313 Bpl WHITE A.R.M. No.1 Coy transferred to CCS 20th attack of	codm
	22/7/17		T/2nd Lieut. S. COOKSON A.S.C. No.4 Coy to 19th Divisional Train. attack of	codm
	23/7/17		Train Hd Qrs., No. 2 & 3 Coys move to CAESTRE Area	codm
CAESTRE Sheet 27 S.E. W.3.a.4.5.	24/7/17		The following letter 4/21st inst, received from the D.D.S.T. 2nd Army. "The Army Commander directs me to convey to all ranks of the A.S.C. (M.T. H.T. & Supply) in the Second Army his great appreciation of the excellent work performed by all branches, which has materially assisted towards the success of the recent operation. Please make known to all ranks under your command an expression of the above."	codm

D.D. & L. London, E.C. A5011 Wt. W.1771/M2035 750,000 5/17 Sch. 53 Forms C.2—0/14

Army Form C. 2118.

WAR DIARY
or
INTELLIGENCE SUMMARY.

(Erase heading not required.)

Instructions regarding War Diaries and Intelligence Summaries are contained in F. S. Regs., Part II. and the Staff Manual respectively. Title pages will be prepared in manuscript.

Place	Date	Hour	Summary of Events and Information	Remarks and references to Appendices
CAESTRE Sheet 27.S.E. W.3.a.4.5.	24 Cent		One R.O. lorry & mule on charge. No. 1 Coy assembling 17th M.V. Coy on L. horse, completes to establishment. Transferred to 52 M.V. Coy 22 horses.	WDW
	25/7		No. 3 Coy move to ZERMEZEELE area. No. 7055307 Cpl GREEN T No. 2 Coy assembled 21 pounds	WDW
	26/7		No. 2 Coy & transport of iron H.Q. move to ZERMEZEELE Area. No. 3 Coy continue move to BRAY DUNES	WDW
	27/7		No. 2 Coy & transport of T.H.Qrs move to LA PANNE. Orderly Room move to WORMHOUDT. 4 Coy move to WORMHOUDT	WDW
LA PANNE Sheet 11. W.15.a.5.2	28/7		Railhead OOSTHOUK. No. 4 Coy move to GHYVELDE.	WDW
	29/7		2 Reinforcements join from Base Depot.	WDW
	30/7		Lt. O.W.M. SHELTON A.S.C. transferred to England, strength of 4 other ranks to England undergo a course of instruction. Motor Transit	WDW

Army Form C. 2118.

WAR DIARY
INTELLIGENCE SUMMARY.
(Erase heading not required.)

Place	Date	Hour	Summary of Events and Information	Remarks and references to Appendices
LA PANNE Sheet 11 W.15.a.6.2	1/10/17		Extract from Orders Gazette 4/10/17. To be Lieut: 2 Lt. C.F. LOEHNER A.S.C. 17.	
	2/10/17		No. T2 SR. 03767 D. BRIEN. R. No. 1 Cy. to Headquarters 2nd Army 18 Chin. Stant of. Authority 2nd Army No. A/2162 of 30/9/17	
	3/10/17		One H.Q. Lorie n charge No. 3 Cy. evacuated 13 Sick. Stant of	
	4/10/17		No. T. 30391 N SCROGGIE C. No. 2 Cy evacuated 2nd evnt. Stant of	
	5/10/17		No. 3 Cy move to ST IDESBALDE.	
	6/10/17		Captain F.V. PERRY A.V.C. attached H.Q. 2th. evacuated to C.C.S. 5th chest of	
	7/10/17		On H.Q. Lorie n charge No. 3 Cy. drive to ST IDESBALDE. Sheet 11. W.10.b.1.6. Train H.Q. Lth. move to ZERMEZEELE. Railway ST IDESBALDE	

No. 1 (Aron) D.D. & L. London E.C. Wt.W1778/M2931 750,000 5/17 Sch. 52 Forms/C2118/14

Army Form C. 2118.

WAR DIARY
or
INTELLIGENCE SUMMARY.
(Erase heading not required.)

Instructions regarding War Diaries and Intelligence Summaries are contained in F. S. Regs., Part II. and the Staff Manual respectively. Title pages will be prepared in manuscript.

Place	Date	Hour	Summary of Events and Information	Remarks and references to Appendices
ST IDES BALDE Shed 11 W10.B.16	8/10/17		One N.C.O. Acre in charge No. 4 Coy. presented 5th hand. Struck off No. 1 Coy. moved from ZERMEZEELE to ST POL SUR MER	[signature]
	9/10/17		No. T/26301 A/Cpl LORIMER F. joined from Base Depot. No. 043479 Sgt. LESLIE A.G. + 1 Rlm. of No. 1 Coy. transferred to 158th A.F.A. Cble in 5th Divn. Authority XV Corps No. A.C/8547/3 of 30/9/17.	[signature]
	10/10/17		Transfer. No. T/330362 Dr. STRINGER J.E. No. 1 Coy. to No. 3 Coy. No. T/36598 Dr. COLLINS E.C. No. 3. to No. 1 Coy with effect from 11th inst.	[signature]
	11/10/17		2 N.C.Os. Acre in charge No. 2 Coy. presented, struck off.	[signature]
	12/10/17		5 Grants awarded 1st G.C. Badge. No. T/057653 Dr. Edinborough R.R. Trans Hd Qts evacuated C.C.S. Struck off.	[signature]
	13/10/17		Immediate Awards. The undermentioned awarded the MILITARY MEDAL for gallantry in the Field on 21/9/17. T4/065205 Dr. H.J.MELLERSH. No. 3 Coy T/35626 Dr. G.E.TAYLOR " 3 "	[signature]

D. D. & I., London, E.C.
(Af011) Wt. W1771/M1093 750,000 5/17 Sch. 82 Forms/C2118/14

WAR DIARY
or
INTELLIGENCE SUMMARY.
(Erase heading not required.)

Army Form C. 2118.

Place	Date	Hour	Summary of Events and Information	Remarks and references to Appendices
ST IDESBALDE W.10.b.1.6	14/10/17		Transfer. No. T/041209 Dr HARVEY C. from Hd Qrs to No 1 Coy. No T/26069 Dr LATCHELL W. No 1 Coy to Lines of Com Hd Qrs.	
	15/10/17		6 Horses received from Remounts. 12 Horses Taken on Strength. S. Transport N.C.Os. confirmed in rank. } Authority - A.S.6. Section 1. Supply N.C.Os. " " } No. 20373 of 12/7/17. S/Sgt O/H 3918 Cpl JOHNSTON E. No. 3 Coy transferred to Hd Qrs 2nd Army + Struck off Strength. Authority ASC Section item No. S/164 of 15/7/17.	
	16/10/17		One G.S. wagon, 2 H.D. Lorries Harness Transferred 14th Brd to 66th D.A.C. Struck off. Authority & Cnfm No. Q.C. 2732/84 of 17	
	17/10/17		One H.D. Lorry No. 69 in charge No. 4 Coy Sent 15 Lines Struck off	
	18/10/17		The undermentioned Promotion to take effect only not to mean Gratuity if rank to promulgate in London Gazette. Officers Lieut M POOLES A.S.C. to be Captain Lieut A.S BLACK A.S.C. to be Captain	

Army Form C. 2118.

WAR DIARY
or
INTELLIGENCE SUMMARY.
(Erase heading not required.)

Instructions regarding War Diaries and Intelligence Summaries are contained in F. S. Regs., Part II. and the Staff Manual respectively. Title pages will be prepared in manuscript.

Place	Date	Hour	Summary of Events and Information	Remarks and references to Appendices
ST. DESBALDE Hut 11 W.10 b.1.6	19/10/17		The H.Q. hose No. 66 in charge No. 2 Coy heat presented 16th strength	
"	20/10/17		No. S.S./704 Sgt. MONTEATH W.13 joined from Base Depot. Taken on strength	
	21/9/17		3 Reinforcements join from Base Depot. No. T.H. 244273 L/Cpl EVANS M. No. 4 Coy to No. 2 Coy.	
	22/10/17		2nd Lt C.M.C. LUFF A.S.C. to be Lieut. Subject to promulgation in London Gazette.	
	23/10/17		Lieut. A.S. BLACK A.S.C. transferred to Indian Army. Strick off from 22nd.	
	24/10/17		Capt. M. POOLES. A.S.C. ceased to perform the duties of Adjutant. 2 Reinforcements (Joiners) join from Base Depot. 1 H.Q. horse received from Remounts. Taken on strength. 2. H.Q. horses + 1 mule in charge No. 1 Coy. presented on 23rd strength off.	
	25/10/17		The Rates received from Remount. 24th inst. Taken on strength.	

Army Form C. 2118.

WAR DIARY
or
INTELLIGENCE SUMMARY.
(Erase heading not required.)

Instructions regarding War Diaries and Intelligence Summaries are contained in F. S. Regs., Part II. and the Staff Manual respectively. Title pages will be prepared in manuscript.

Place	Date	Hour	Summary of Events and Information	Remarks and references to Appendices
ST IDESBALDE Sheet 11. W.10.b.6.	25/10/17		Coy. One H.Q. Lorry No. 10 in charge of Spr. T/T026131 L/Cpl SAWDON F. 2nd Crew struck of to 3 Coy. T.H.M.N. to 3 Coy. T/330362 D'r STRINGER J.E. No. 3 Coy to T.H.M.N S/353373 Pte HACKING G. No. 2 Coy to No. 3 Coy.	[signature]
	26/10/17		One H.Q. Lorry No. 7 in charge of No. 4 Coy died. Struck off	[signature]
	27/10/17		One H.Q. Lorry No. 118 in charge of No. 3 Coy died. Struck off	[signature]
	28/10/17		One H.Q. Lorry No. 25 in charge of No. H Coy died 27th Struck of No. 4 Coy move to Sheet 19. C.29.c.11. TETEGHEM.	[signature]
	29/10/17		Train Hd Qtrs. move Rue de Liege ROSENDAEL No. 1 Coy move to Sheet 19. D.28.d.3.3. GHYVELDE No. 2 Coy move to Sheet 19. H.11.c.3.5 All Officers men on leave recalled. 28th inst	[signature]
ROSENDAEL	30/10/17		Lieut B & M ANDREW A.S.C. No. 3 Coy transport to R.E.'s struck off	[signature]

WAR DIARY
or
INTELLIGENCE SUMMARY.
(Erase heading not required.)

Army Form C. 2118.

Place	Date	Hour	Summary of Events and Information	Remarks and references to Appendices
ROSENDAEL	30/10/17		Lieut. C.F. LOCHNER. A.S.C. T.H.&K. struck off strength. On M.O. Leave in charge Ho. & Coy. remainder (Strength of)	
	31/10/17		Captain S.C.A. HAYS joined from 42nd Div. Train. Main H.Q. Lines & 1 L.B. received from Remounts. Sgt 060466 Cpl ROSSER J.O. & No. T/23832 D. SAMSON F.T. HH. &Tr. reposted from Central Purchase Board. No. M/245167 A/Cpl TAIT J.J. & MAXWELL Car No. 29750 transferred to H Army T.S.C. struck off. No. M/047030 Pte TALBOT. E.G. & SUNBEAM Car No. 1637 joined from H Army T.S.C. taken on strength reposted to T.H.&Tr.	

J.D. Parker Capt.
Commdg H1 & Div. Train

WAR DIARY
or
INTELLIGENCE SUMMARY.

(Erase heading not required.)

Army Form C. 2118.

41 D. Train

No 23

Place	Date	Hour	Summary of Events and Information	Remarks and references to Appendices
CAMPOSAMPIERO ITALY	1/3/18		2nd Lieut J. BOOTH ASC attached to 23rd Div Train	MR
	2/3/18		H Qrs Train close down r enhained CAMPOSAMPIERO 8.15 am	MR
	3/4/18		Train Journey.	MR
	5/3/18		Arrived DOULLENS & march to LUCHEUX arriving 10 pm	MR
	6/3/18		Train office opened 2/Lieut J Cavanagh ASC, 2/Lieut MR J. Savill ASC joined from 2nd ASC Base Depot HTS	MR
LUCHEUX FRANCE	7/3/18		2nd Lieut J BOOTH ASC transferred XIV Corps & struck off. Lieut B.A. EMBY ASC posted to T.H.Qrs	MR
	8/3/18		Transfers Capt M/S POLLARD URQUHART ASC from 4 Coy to 3 Coy as SO.123 9 Bde. Capt E.H. TRUITER ASC from 3 Coy to 4 Coy as SO.124 9 Bde	MR
	9/3/18		N° Tn/094229 Pte WHITESIDE. W. rejoined from CCS & taken on Strength. SM/092289 Cpl ASHWORTH. J rejoined from BASE "	MR
	10/3/18		Usual Routine	MR
	11/3/18		Awarded 1st G.C. Badge N° S1/SR/412 a/Cpl Eardley W. E T.H.Q. M2/033116 " Jk " " Sh/055166 " Kerr " Th/054781 Dr Arkle W.H. 3 Coy W/143066 Dr Sad Noble H.W.H. " T3/027001 " Scully J H.	MR

Army Form C. 2118.

WAR DIARY
INTELLIGENCE SUMMARY
(Erase heading not required.)

Place	Date	Hour	Summary of Events and Information	Remarks and references to Appendices
LUCHEUX FRANCE	12/3/18	-	Usual Routine	M.P
	13/3/18	-	No. TS/6701 Dvr S.Sgt BRODIE R. rejoined this formation from C.C.S. & posted to No.1 Coy.	M.P
	14/3/18	-	No. T4/251465 Dvr BROWN R.M. No.2 Coy transferred 5th class struck off	M.P
	15/3/18		Usual routine. Dvr LORIMER F. struck off	M.P
	16/3/18		Appointments: T/7619 Dvr (C.S.M) SCARRATT F.) appointed L/Cpl. T/8518 Dvr (A/Sgt) VOSPER G.R.S) Authority A.C.I. Vol. No.1 T/22536 Dvr (Cpl) CHIDGEY H.) A.J. 309/1918	M.P
	17/3/18		No. T2/13472 Dvr GORTON C. transferred 1st Band. struck of	M.P
	18/3/18		No. T3/35644 Dvr BRAIB transferred to H.O. Offrs 123rd 2d Btle. Struck of No. T/26301 A/Cpl LORIMER F. transfer to permanent grade Sewr	M.P
	19/3/18		No. T4/251796 to L/M. IRVING A. appointed A/S.Sgt. on transfer to 46 D.A. Train authorty. A.S.C. P.O.B/1146397 dt 14/3/11	M.P
	20/3/18		No. T4/251796 A.S.S.M. IRVING A. posted to H6 D.A.D. Train. Struck of	M.P

WAR DIARY
or
INTELLIGENCE SUMMARY

Army Form C. 2118.

Place	Date	Hour	Summary of Events and Information	Remarks and references to Appendices
FRANCE	21/3/18		Coy Hd Qts move to BRESLE	M.P.
			No. 1 Coy " " BAVELINCOURT	
			" 2 " " " RIBEMONT	
			" 3 " " " BOUZINCOURT	
			" 4 " " " NAVIEVILLE	
	22/3/18		Coy Hd Qts + Coys move to ACHIET LE PETIT	M.P.
	23/3/18		No. T/110334 Dr BURLING. J. No. 4 Coy transferred to 724 L.F.M.H.D. 20 Enemy + friendly aircraft overhead	M.P.
			One H.D. Lorry in charge No. 1 Coy encountered 20 Enemy aircraft.	
	24/3/18		Camp C killed from 3 pm to 4.30 pm No. T/94492 Dr BRIDSON. R.D. wounded. 2 - H.D. Horses + 2 G.S. wagons in charge of No. 2 Coy destroyed + 1 bicycle in charge of No. 1 Coy destroyed. The wagons were loaded with rations & were totally destroyed.	M.P.
			Camp moved at 5.30 pm to field in ACHIET LE PETIT — BUCQUOY Road.	
	25/3/18		Coy Hd Qts Coy move to BIENVILLER au Boc. moved again at 5 pm to ST-AMAND.	M.P.

Army Form C. 2118.

WAR DIARY
or
INTELLIGENCE SUMMARY
(Erase heading not required.)

Instructions regarding War Diaries and Intelligence Summaries are contained in F. S. Regs., Part II. and the Staff Manual respectively. Title Pages will be prepared in manuscript.

Place	Date	Hour	Summary of Events and Information	Remarks and references to Appendices
FRANCE	26/3/18		About 10 am rumour received that enemy cavalry had been sighted in the vicinity. DHQ and 1st Line Transport together with Some Coys move from HQ at BAILLEULVAL	MP
	27/3/18		Remain at BAILLEULVAL. No 1 Coy move to join 62nd Division	MP
	28/3/18		Move to GOMBREMETZ.	MP
	29/3/18		Move to AUTHIE.	MP
	30/3/18		1st MAC + 2,3rd Coys at AUTHIE	MP
	31/3/18		Six reinforcement joined from Base Depot 24 Divl Train strength. 2/Lt PRL SAVILL admitted 135th Ambce 24 Divn (accidentally injured)	MP

MP Noel Capron
fr. COMMDG. 41st DIVNL. TRAIN, A.S.C.

WAR DIARY or INTELLIGENCE SUMMARY

Army Form C. 2118

Place	Date	Hour	Summary of Events and Information	Remarks and references to Appendices
AUTHIE FRANCE	1/7/18		No. T/8951 A/L/Cpl. JOBSON, T.E. promoted A/L. Cpl. 28/7/11 Authority: AsC Pt.I/8625/296. No. T/23791 L/S STEWART A.C. No. 2 Cy promoted L/Cpl. struck off	MP MP
HALLOY	2/7/18		2nd Md Ak. moved to HALLOY	MP
STEENVOORDE	3/7/18		2nd Md Ak Hqrs. open at STEENVOORDE. No. 2 Cy. billets PETIT HOUVIN at 7. P.m.	MP
"	4/7/18		No. T/36248 D. THOMAS G.H. No. 3 Cy admitted P. while on leave in U.K. [25/7/18] No. 2 Cy. billets PESELHOEK 9am. Struck off PESELHOEK 11.15 am No. 3 Cy. billets PETIT HOUVIN 2.30 am & billets at PESELHOEK 4. 0 Pm No. 4 Cy. billets PETIT HOUVIN 6.0. am & billets at PESELHOEK	MP
"	5/7/18		2 H.Q. Lorry in charge No. 1 Cy. Proceeded 26 Bn. struck off.	MP
"	6/7/18		No. T/73455 L/N FRY. H. No. 3 Cy admitted P. 4/7/18. struck off.	MP

WAR DIARY
or
INTELLIGENCE SUMMARY
(Erase heading not required.)

Army Form C. 2118

Instructions regarding War Diaries and Intelligence Summaries are contained in F. S. Regs., Part II. and the Staff Manual respectively. Title Pages will be prepared in manuscript.

Place	Date	Hour	Summary of Events and Information	Remarks and references to Appendices
STEENVOORDE	7/7/18		Q Drivers, 18 H.D Lorries & G.S. wagon, surplus to establishment, owing to the reorganisation of Coy Estb., struck off the strength. Authority 3rd Army No. S.Q./191 of 2/7/18.	M.P
	8/7/18		No. T3/027085 H/Cpl PARKER W. No. 2 Coy. reduced to perm. grade of Driver, forfeits 1 G.C Badge.	M.P
	9/7/18		One N.O. Lorie in charge No. 1 Coy. destroyed.	M.P
	10/7/18		Coy. move to RYDE Camp Area. G.4.a.3.0. Sheet 28.	M.P
G.4.a.3.0. Sheet 28.	11/7/18		4 Drivers, 8 H.D Lorries, 1 G.S. wagon, owing to reduction of M.G Batt., transferred to No. 1 Coy. Lain.	M.P
	12/7/18		No. T/356267 Pte Stebber D. No. 2 Coy. awarded 10 Emil. struck off	M.P

WAR DIARY
or
INTELLIGENCE SUMMARY
(Erase heading not required.)

Army Form C. 2118

Place	Date	Hour	Summary of Events and Information	Remarks and references to Appendices
G.H.Q. 3.0.	13/7/18		No. S/35556/76 Pte HAINSWORTH. A.E. No. 1 Coy returned to Base Depot as Overland-Typist. 24/7/18. Struck off.	MP
	14/7/18		No. T/044653 Cpl MULCAHY. C.F. No. 1 Coy. appointed a/C.S.M. from 22/3/18. Authority Warrant Reserve. No CR/49606/C. of 2/7/18 & ASC Section No. ASC P26/1146327 of 10/7/18.	MP
	15/7/18		No. T/044653 a/C.S.M. MULCAHY. C.F. No. 1 Coy. to No. 6 Coy + Coy.	MP
	16/7/18		No. T/3/026231 Pte McNEE. D. No. 2 Coy. warranted 13 Divn. struck off.	MP
	17/7/18		Railhead PESELHOEK. The following casualties occurred at Railhead, owing to Shellfire. No. T/4/094206 Dr CROCKER. S.J. killed. No. S/4/043970 S. Sjt. KEEFE. W. wounded. " S/4/2242 Corpl. BARON. W. " T/3/627003 Pte. MURRAY. M. " M/37205 Pte. MITTEN. J. "	MP

WAR DIARY
or
INTELLIGENCE SUMMARY.

(Erase heading not required.)

Army Form C. 2118.

Instructions regarding War Diaries and Intelligence Summaries are contained in F.S. Regs., Part II. and the Staff Manual respectively. Title pages will be prepared in manuscript.

Place	Date	Hour	Summary of Events and Information	Remarks and references to Appendices
G.4.a 3.0.	18/7/15		Railhead PROVEN. 6 N.C.O.'s & men killed by shell fire 17th struck off strength. No 24/10247 Pte Burgess J. No 2 Coy admitted R. table on leave in U.K. Struck off strength from 24/7/15. 3 N.C.O.'s & men wounded 17 ervs struck off. 1 G.S. wagon destroyed 17 ervs	M.O.
	19/7/15		No. S4/043970 S/Sgt. KEEFE W. No. 3 Coy. invalided C.C.S. 17 ervs struck off. S4/042242 Corpl BARON W. " 2 do 13/027003 Driver MURRAY M. - 2 do	M.O.
	20/7/15		No. T2/027039 Sgt. ROBERTSON W.P. } No 2 Coy invalided C.C.S. 16 emi. struck off. S2/016374 Pte BATCHELOR G. }	M.O.
	21/7/15		No. T2/014927 Dr GOLDSWORTHY A. invalided C.C.S. 16 emi. struck off.	M.O.

WAR DIARY
or
INTELLIGENCE SUMMARY.
(Erase heading not required.)

Army Form C. 2118.

Place	Date	Hour	Summary of Events and Information	Remarks and references to Appendices
G.4.a.3.0.	22/8		Board of Enquiry assembled in office of No. 2 Coy. to inquire into the illegal absence of No. 33136 Dr Maloney J. No. 4 Coy. Presedent Capt. C. Tripp. A.S.C. Members { Lieut. B.A. Emby " 2 Lieut. J.B. Aston "	MP
	23/8		Two H.Q. Lorries in charge of No. 3 Coy. evacuated 21 Lieut. Colonels Off.	MP
	24/8		No. T2 03775 Dr Wood A.C. No. 4 Coy. transferred to 124 Fd Bde H.Q. 23 Divn. Cotwels Off. No. T4 110334 Dr Burling J. from 12th Bde to No. 4 Coy. 23 Divn. taken on strength. No. T37205 Dr Mitten J. No. 1 Coy. evacuated 6.6.U. 23 Divn. Cotwels Off.	MP
	25/8		One Rider in charge No. 4 Coy. evacuated 23 Divn. Cotwels Off. No. T110570 Cpl. Young G.R. No. 3 Coy. evacuated C.C.S. 19 Divn. Cotwels Off.	MP
	26/8		1 H.Qk + 2 3 + Coy move to Sheet 28. A. 16. a. 8. w. No. 33136 Dr Maloney J. No. 4 Coy. Having deserted in Cotwels Off absent from 22 Instant.	MP

WAR DIARY
or
INTELLIGENCE SUMMARY.
(Erase heading not required.)

Army Form C. 2118.

Place	Date	Hour	Summary of Events and Information	Remarks and references to Appendices
Sheet 28. A.16.a.8.4	27/8		Train shifted move to Sheet 27. F.21.d.1.2. No. 2 Coy move to Sheet 27. F.28.a.4.1. No. 3 " " " 27. F.28.a.4.5. No. 4 " " " 27. F.28.a.4.5.	M.O
	28/8		No. T3/9333 L/Cpl. MAHER P. No.1 Coy evacuated C.C.S. 23 2nd Pltnck yy 9 Horses sent to Base Depot. Taken on strength. 17 MD horses + 3 Riders received from Remounts.	M.O
	29/8		Casualties. The following casualties occurred at Railhead PROVEN T/2nd Lt. S.G. ALDOUS A.S.C wounded " N PARKES A. " T/4 094168 T/4 057205 N WHITEFORD J. " 3 MD horses killed 1 G.S. wagon destroyed.	M.O
	30/8		2 horses join from Base Depot, taken on strength. Railhead ST OMER.	M.O

A. Foster Captain
COMMDG 31st DIVNL TRAIN, A.S.C.

Army Form C. 2118.

WAR DIARY
or
INTELLIGENCE SUMMARY.
(Erase heading not required.)

Instructions regarding War Diaries and Intelligence Summaries are contained in F.S. Regs., Part II. and the Staff Manual respectively. Title pages will be prepared in manuscript.

Place	Date	Hour	Summary of Events and Information	Remarks and references to Appendices
Abel 21 F.21.d.1.2	1/5/18		No. T/27831 Pte CASSIDY. B. No. 3 Cy. admitted R while on leave in U.K. Struck off strength from 31/3/18.	WSM
	2/5/18		On H.Q. Leave No. 61 on leave No. 1 Cy. proceeded. Struck W.	WSM
	3/5/18		No. T/094168 Pte PARKES A. No. 1 Cy. proceeded 66d. 29th Struck W. "T/057205" Pte WHITEFORD J. do.	WSM
	4/5/18		Board of Officers assemble at No. 2 & 3rd Cys to examine certain articles of clothing held in charge, to determine the condition of same. Members { President. Capt W.S MAILE ASC Lieut. B.A. EMISY " 2/Lt. J. CAVANAGH " }	WSM
	5/5/18		Appointments No. T/35894 A/Cpl SMITH J.E. No. 3 Cy. to be T/Cpl. Authority " T/056856 Dvr KENT A.T. " 3 " to be a/T/Cpl ASC. P.29/264/21 " T/065218 " HURST R.J. " 2 " " to be T/Cpl.) of 24/4/18.	WSM
	6/5/18		No. T/22536 A/Cpl CHIDGEY. H. No. 3 Cy. transferred to No. 2 Cy. on Comds from Base Depot. Taken on Strength.	WSM

Army Form C. 2118.

WAR DIARY
or
INTELLIGENCE SUMMARY.
(Erase heading not required.)

Instructions regarding War Diaries and Intelligence Summaries are contained in F.S. Regs., Part II. and the Staff Manual respectively. Title pages will be prepared in manuscript.

Place	Date	Hour	Summary of Events and Information	Remarks and references to Appendices
Ded. 21 F 21 d.1.2.	7/5/18		No. S/3829H Pte FOOTE E. No.1 Cy seconded 66s. (Struck off from & rnl. " S4/060466 Corpl. ROSSIER J.O. No.2 Cy. transferred to No.3 Cy. " S2/016383 Pte COWLING W. No. + Cy " " " 2 Cy.	COSM
	8/5/18		Appointments T/3/027083 Sergt GIBBS. W. No.1 Cy to be Tempt appopl. " " T/3/316 Sergt BROWN. W.H. " " " " " One H.Q. Lyne in Lorge No.1 Cy. died & Gnrl. (Struck off)	COSM
	9/5/18		Captain L.W. BROWNE C.F. attached No.1 Cy. proceeded to Ypres to D.A.C.G. CALAIS on 8th Innel. (Struck off)	COSM
	10/5/18		One Rider + one H.Q. in Lorge No.1 Cy. seconded 20th. (Struck off)	
	11/5/18		3 Reinforcements from from K.S.C. Base Depart. No. T4/083268 D. PEATTIE T. No.2 Cy. transferred to Hd.Qrs. 122nd I. Bde. (Struck off)	COSM

WAR DIARY
or
INTELLIGENCE SUMMARY.
(Erase heading not required.)

Army Form C. 2118.

Place	Date	Hour	Summary of Events and Information	Remarks and references to Appendices
Sheet 27 F.21.d.1.2	12/5/18		6 Grooms arrived 1st G.H.Bde. No. T/35651 N Applebee H. joined from R. Potal to 3 Cy. 1 SLD Loose on Large No. 1 Cy. arrested. (Strength off.)	COSM
	13/5/18		No. T/026059 N Whyte J. No. 4 Cy. evacuated hosp. 11/5. (Strength off.) 2nd Lieut. S.G. Aldous ASC. No. 2 Cy. evacuated to England (wounded) on 4th inst. Strength off.	COSM
	14/5/18		No. T/065206 N George H. } of No. 2 Cy. " T/024826 " Hughes W. } transferred to 138th Fd. Amb. T/294419 " Taylor J. No. S/389153 Pte Wason A. (clerk) } S/056848 Pte Gosden W.A. (drau) joined from New Depot.	COSM
	15/5/18		2nd Lieut. A.W. Roulston A.S.C. joined from Base Depot on 14th inst. Proc. the name to Louis Chateau Enclose Sheet 27/F.16.d.9.0.	COSM
Sheet 27 F.16.d.9.0.	16/5/18		Extract from Supplement to London Gazette of 14/5/18 T/Captain B.W. Parker ASC. to be T/Major T/Lieut. R. Harris ASC. to be T/Captain	COSM

WAR DIARY
of
INTELLIGENCE SUMMARY.
(Erase heading not required.)

Army Form C. 2118.

Place	Date	Hour	Summary of Events and Information	Remarks and references to Appendices
Abeel 27 F.16.d.9.0.	16/7/18	Conclusion	**Promotions** T/4079 A/C.S.M. BAXTER C. No 1 Coy Promoted C.S.M.s from 1/3/17 T/3/026737 A/Cpl SAWDON F. " " " Cnpl. 13/11/17 T/4/198191 A/L/Cpl JONES S.G. 2 " " L/Cpl. 2/7/11 Authority :- ASC P29/12953 of 12/5/18 T/4/142113 A/Sgt LUNN A.E. No 1 Coy Promoted S/Sgt from 28/1/17 Authority :- ASC P21/8526/296 of 11/5/18	
	17/5/18		No. T/3/025369 Pte FRANKS J. No 1 Coy + 5 H.Q. Lorries, wounded by bombs dropped by Locale airerafe on night of 1/6/18. 5 H.Q. Lorries received from Remounts. No. S/044873 Sgt BARKER G.A. No 1 Coy transferred 1st M.T. (Church of England) Sgt S/044169 Cpl KIMPTON F. changed from "Sgt" to "Pte." the category of from May 1915. Authority :- ASC W187/856 of 13/5/18.	
	18/5/18		T/2nd Lieut. P.R.L. SAVILLE ASC found to be unfit for general service for 3 months struck off strength on change from 3 June	

WAR DIARY
or
INTELLIGENCE SUMMARY.

Army Form C. 2118.

Place	Date	Hour	Summary of Events and Information	Remarks and references to Appendices
Sheet 27 F.16.d.9.0	1918 19/5		Normal routine	worn
	20/5		Normal routine	worn
	21/5		F/Lieut W.F PICKFORD. A/S joined from Base Depot posted to H.Q. & Coy. The following attended a Course of Instruction in Stockholm gunnery at II Corps School and classified as stated: T/4/065307 Cpl. GREEN. F. — Instructional Ability — Good T/4/057709 " FISHER.T. — do — Fair T/4/060725 " SANDERSON.J.H. — do — Fair.	worn
	22/5		No. T/3/025369 Pte FRANKS. J. evacuated to 66.L.(wounded) on 16th inst. " T/4/210251 " WELLER. F.G. joined from Base Depot on 11th inst. " T/4/210251 " WELLER. F.G. evacuated to 66 J. 15th inst. Struck off.	worn
	23/5		F/2nd Lieut. A.W. ROULSTON A/S posted to H.Q. & Coy. from 4 Coy.	worn

Army Form C. 2118.

WAR DIARY
or
INTELLIGENCE SUMMARY.
(Erase heading not required.)

Place	Date	Hour	Summary of Events and Information	Remarks and references to Appendices
Deal 27 F.16.d9.0	24/7/18		No. S/17395 A/Sgt. BAWDEN G. posted from No. 3 Base Supply Depot — Posted to No. 1 Coy. No. S/17395 A/Sgt BAWDEN G appointed A/S/Sgt, dept, with pay from 25/7/18. Authority: A.S.C. P28/12614/F.7. $\frac{35}{2}$ of 15-5/18	
	25/7		Re-engagement Leave. The following N.C.O's men were granted re-engagement leave of absence as re-engaged, in date as stated. CH7 286 A. SAWDON J. 5-8/16 T/15737 - MANLEY P.K. 26/7/17 T/244373 H/Cpl. EVANS M. 16/8/17 T/251/86 CSM IRVING A. 13/9/17 T/237611 Cpl. RUSSELL A.L. 4/7/18 T/20458 A/Sgt. STIRRUP J. 18/7/18 T/22558 A/Cpl BRIDGEY H 25/7/18 T/250123 Cpl STOREY E. 13/7/18 T/16515 McLOUGHLIN M. 15-7-18	
	26/7		Usual routine	

Army Form C. 2118.

WAR DIARY
or
INTELLIGENCE SUMMARY.
(Erase heading not required.)

Instructions regarding War Diaries and Intelligence Summaries are contained in F.S. Regs., Part II. and the Staff Manual respectively. Title pages will be prepared in manuscript.

Place	Date	Hour	Summary of Events and Information	Remarks and references to Appendices
Sheet 27. F.16.d.9.0.	27/10		5 reinforcements joined from A.S.C. Base Depot.	W.W.
	28/10		No. 7207 Pte Kelly J.J. No. 3 Coy awarded 1st div. F.P. 2 - forfeits 1 G.C. Badge.	W.W.
	29/10		**Cranville** The following casualties occurred about 7.30 p.m. owing to a Shell falling into a small tent.

T/4/76133 C.Q.M.S. BARRETT W.F. killed
T/3/022987 Sgt BULL W "
S/4/070116 " NAISMITH A.N. "
SS/704 " MONTEATH W.B. died of wounds
T/4/044570 " BULMER J.W. "
T/4/198191 2/Cpl JONES S.G. died of wounds
T/4/185437 L/Sgt. LUGG J.H. killed
T/4/294578 " HOPPER J.R. "
T/355519 " PERKIN I.W. "

These N.C.O.'s men were buried on 30th inst in Dozinghem Adv. M.C. Cemetery. Sheet 27. F.11.a.5.7. Plot 14 Row G. T/4/198191 2/Cpl JONES S.G. buried on Sheet 27 L.10.b.35. | W.W. |

Army Form C. 2118.

WAR DIARY
or
INTELLIGENCE SUMMARY.
(Erase heading not required.)

Instructions regarding War Diaries and Intelligence Summaries are contained in F. S. Regs., Part II. and the Staff Manual respectively. Title pages will be prepared in manuscript.

Place	Date	Hour	Summary of Events and Information	Remarks and references to Appendices
Nov 27 F.16.d.9.0	30/4		One N.C.O. sent on leave to Angl. No. 1 Coy. remained.	
	31/5/18		Captain R. Harris A.S.C. proceeded to join 58th Div. Trans. for duty.	
			No. 1 Coy. entrained at DOULLENS on 14 Lorries for the area & detrained at WAAVENBURG. 15 9/6.	

W.S. Marker Capt.
Commdg. 412 Div. Train

D. D. & L., London, E.C.
(A8001) Wt. W17771/M2031 750,000 5/17 Sch. 58 Forms/C2118/14

Army Form C. 2118.

41 D Train Vol 26

WAR DIARY
INTELLIGENCE SUMMARY.
(Erase heading not required.)

Instructions regarding War Diaries and Intelligence Summaries are contained in F. S. Regs., Part II. and the Staff Manual respectively. Title pages will be prepared in manuscript.

Place	Date	Hour	Summary of Events and Information	Remarks and references to Appendices
Bool 27. F16.d.9.0	1/1/18		No. T/36581 A/Cpl TOWELL F.M presented C.C.S. 29th. Shoots of Honour Award. Extract from London Gazette Supplement of 30/11. Mentioned in Dispatch.	MP
	2/1/18		No. T/2018 A/L LAKIN W. No. 3 Cy rejoined C.C.S. 29th. Shoots of T/H 057326 L/L WILSON J.F. " " 2nd " T/Captain G.H. COLEGRAVE A.S.C. T/3119 SSM F. EYCOTT	MP
	3/1/18		No. 2. 3 & 4 Cy & Train HQ transport proceed by road 2nd Army Training Area	MP
	4/1/18		No. 2 Cy arrive BLUE MAISON " 3 " " KINDERSELCK " 4 " " E. of CROME ST. & HQ. NIEURLET.	MP

WAR DIARY or **INTELLIGENCE SUMMARY.**

Army Form C. 2118.

Place	Date	Hour	Summary of Events and Information	Remarks and references to Appendices
NIEURLET FRANCE	5/11		On 1129 Lorre in charge No 1 Coy recruited 27 Salb.	M.P.
	6/11		No. M2/079874 Pte FENWICK J.H. & Sunbeam Car No 54163 Joined from H.Q. M.T. Coy on 30th ult. vice No. M2/076902 Pte HARKNESS W.T. & Sunbeam Car No. 1637 recruited to 3Brace + return off.	M.P.
			No. T/t. 245889 6 A.M. Sgt. JOHNSTON L.A.) Joined from T/t 237471 Sgt. SCOTT J.E.) Base Depot T/t 237472 SCOTT W.P.	
	17/11		Probation. No. T/114568 Sgt. (T.S.S.M.) DUGGAN H.J. placed on Probation in the rank of A/Sgt R.R. Auth: C.D. 26 of 15/11. Saw H.Q. Lorre in charge No. 2 Coy recruited S/Lieut. Ifo. from H.Q. Alk move to the Chateau Grounds EPERLECQUES.	M.P.

WAR DIARY
INTELLIGENCE SUMMARY

Army Form C. 2118.

(Erase heading not required.)

Place	Date	Hour	Summary of Events and Information	Remarks and references to Appendices
EPERLECQUES France	8/1		No. 4 Coy. move to HERICAT. He remains of the late Sgt. Bakewi Wm. T. Army S70 burned at ESQUELBECQUES Military Cemetery (New) 30/8. C.O. inspected 1st Line transport of 124th Coy RASC: No.1 Coy arrive RUMINGHEM AREA.	MP
	9/1		One N.C.O. have a large No. 1 Coy killed by a bomb in 5 tons. No. S/090712 Sgt. STEWART A. } Injured from - S/146290 " GOODMAN A } Norse Depot 8 tons + Division joined from New Depot the day No. T/9604 S/KELLY J.J. No. 369 recounted C.6.d. 5th inst.	MP
			Honours Awards. Extract from London Gazette Supplement of 8/1 Awarded the Military Cross. - Capt. T.V. FLEMING RASC. Awarded the Meritorious Services Medal. No. T/213880 ASM. L.A. DUDLEY. RASC.	MP

WAR DIARY
or
INTELLIGENCE SUMMARY.
(Erase heading not required.)

Army Form C. 2118.

Place	Date	Hour	Summary of Events and Information	Remarks and references to Appendices
EPERLECQUES	10/6/18		No. 4 Coy move to BONNINGUES-Les-ARDRES	M.P
FRANCE			No. 3 Coy move to St MARTIN-AU-LAERT	
			No. T/145168 F.o.S.M. DUGGAN H.J. No.1 Coy awarded the Long Service Good Conduct Medal (with gratuity). (Army Order April 1918)	
	11/6/18		C.O. inspects the transport of the 41st Batt. M.G. Corps.	M.P
	12/6/18		C.O. inspects the transport of 139 & 140 st Fd. Amb.	M.P
	13/6/18		No. T/057781 A/ ARKLE W.H No. 3 Coy evacuated No. 4 Stat.y H. 10 Ens.	M.P
			" 54/060516 Pte COLE H.M. " 3 " do	
			" T/043678 A/ HARDMAN E. " 3 " do	
			21 O.Ranks awarded 1st G.C. Badge.	

WAR DIARY
or
INTELLIGENCE SUMMARY.
(Erase heading not required.)

Army Form C. 2118.

Place	Date	Hour	Summary of Events and Information	Remarks and references to Appendices
EPERLECQUES FRANCE	14/7/18		Reorganization	M.P
	15/7/18		No. T/086603 Dr GWYNNE No. 1 Cy invalided to No. 11 C.C.S. 8th inst. Re 11/9 Loss on large No. 1 Cy. invalided 12 inst.	M.P
	16/7/18		No. T/198381 A/Sgt REDSHAW J.E. joined from Base Depot.	M.P
	17/7/18		No. S/389153 Pte WASON A. No. 1 Cy invalided to A.S.C. Base depot on 16th inst. for transit to England on compassionate grounds.	M.P
	18/7/18		T/2nd Lieut. R.S. PEACOCK ASC joined from No. 1 Army Ann. (Horse) Cy on 17th inst. Order No. 3 Cy. No. T/062099 W PATTISON H. No. 1 Cy invalided 15th inst.	M.P
	19/7/18		C/O inspected 1st Line transport 122 I.B.C.	M.P

A5834 Wt.W4973/M657 750,000 8/16 D. D. & L. Ltd. Forms/C.2118/13.

Army Form C. 2118.

WAR DIARY
or
INTELLIGENCE SUMMARY.
(Erase heading not required.)

Instructions regarding War Diaries and Intelligence Summaries are contained in F.S. Regs., Part II. and the Staff Manual respectively. Title pages will be prepared in manuscript.

Place	Date	Hour	Summary of Events and Information	Remarks and references to Appendices
EPERLECQUES FRANCE	20/6		No. T/23419 A/Hilton E No. 2 Coy transferred to Hilton 122 Inf. Bde.	MP
	21/6		Usual routine. C/O inspected 1st Line transport of 19th Middlesex Regt. (Pioneer) 1st Army	MP
	22/6		No. T/244778 A/Cpl Wheal C. joined from Base Depot.	MP
	23/6		No. S/146104 Sgt Halliday W.H. joined from Base Depot.	MP
	24/6		C/O inspected 1st Line transport of 123rd Inf. Bde.	MP
	25/6		Oran Hd. Qrs. transport moved to LEDERZEELE No. 1 Coy moved to ZEGGERS CAPPEL Area " 2 " " " RUBROUCK Area " 3 " " " ST MOMELIN " " 4 " " " LEDERZEELE "	MP

Army Form C. 2118.

WAR DIARY
or
INTELLIGENCE SUMMARY.
(Erase heading not required.)

Instructions regarding War Diaries and Intelligence Summaries are contained in F. S. Regs., Part II. and the Staff Manual respectively. Title pages will be prepared in manuscript.

Place	Date	Hour	Summary of Events and Information	Remarks and references to Appendices
EPERLECQUES FRANCE	26/9		Journal Off. & Transport went to OUDERZEELE	MP
			No. 1 Coy move to WATON FRANCE Sheet 27 K 21. d. 3 4	
			" 2 " " " Sheet 27. J 22. d. 3. 4.	
			" 3 " " " " 27 H 23 b. 5. 0	
			" 4 " " " " 27 J 26 A F 8	
OUDERZEELE FRANCE	27/9		1 H.Q. horse + 1 Rider received from Remount 24 train	MP
			The following supplies to established proceeded to A.H.T. Depot ABBEVILLE on 25th inst. are struck off the strength	
			No. T. 28225 D. VINALL A.M. No. 1 Coy	
			2 H.Q. horses " " "	
			1 G.S. wagon " " "	
	28/9		Supplies drawn by H.Q. from STEENVOORDE. Mules rations	MP
	29/9		Supplies drawn by H.Q. from STEENVOORDE.	MP

Army Form C. 2118.

WAR DIARY
or
INTELLIGENCE SUMMARY.
(Erase heading not required.)

Place	Date	Hour	Summary of Events and Information	Remarks and references to Appendices
OUDEZEELE FRANCE	30/9/18		No. 1499 Pte HAGUE 19th Middlesex Regt. allt. to No. 1 Coy. b/o course of instruction on "Hot Chassis" from 28th. No. 3 Coy. move to Sheet 27/K.21.d.7.4.	MT
			Epidemic of Influenza prevailed during month.	MP
			Captain & Adjt. M. POOLES & Capt. E.H. TRUTER are admitted to No. 64 C.C.S. on 25th inst. (sick).	

[signature]
COMMDG. 41st DIVNL. TRAIN, A.S.C.

Army Form C. 2118.

WAR DIARY
or
INTELLIGENCE SUMMARY.
(Erase heading not required.)

Instructions regarding War Diaries and Intelligence Summaries are contained in F.S. Regs., Part II. and the Staff Manual respectively. Title pages will be prepared in manuscript.

Place	Date	Hour	Summary of Events and Information	Remarks and references to Appendices
OUDEZEELE FRANCE	1/7/18		Nos. 2 + 4 Coy move to Sheet 27/K26.c.3.4 + K27.c.3.0, respectively	M.P.
	2/7/18		T/9333 S/L/Cpl MAHER P. reported from 13 Base Depot. 1st M.J. Jones + T/2 Drivers 1st 12 from Base Depot. Captain arg. M. Poole discharged to duty from No. 64 G.C.S.	M.P.
			Lieut. H.S. OK. went to Sheet 27/K.21.C.8.5. Captain W.S. MAILE admitted to 1st Aust. C.C.S. (sick) in 1 mot.	M.P.
K21.b.8.5 Sheet 27.	3/7/18		1 Car H.Q. + 1 Rider to large No. 1 (G) unmounted. No. 2 Coy move to K.27.a. 3.10. Sheet 27.	M.P.
	4/7/18		2 w/o N.C.O. Liars to Large No. 1 (G) unmounted.	M.P.
	5/7/18		No. S/17395 2/S. Sgt. BAWDEN G. No. 1 (G) returned to Base Depot. Surplus to establishment. Struck off 1st G.C. Bndge. awarded to T/SR.O2732 N. POWELL J.J. No. 1 (G) cancelled.	M.P.
	6/7/18		Lieut. G.M.G. LUFF A.S.C. proceeded to England to undergo a course of instruction in Infantry duties. Struck off T/Lt. No. 210346 N. SHARPE B. No. 3 (G) transferred to 723 Gs H.Q.	M.P.

Army Form C. 2118.

WAR DIARY
INTELLIGENCE SUMMARY.
(Erase heading not required.)

Instructions regarding War Diaries and Intelligence Summaries are contained in F. S. Regs., Part II. and the Staff Manual respectively. Title pages will be prepared in manuscript.

Place	Date	Hour	Summary of Events and Information	Remarks and references to Appendices
K.21.b & 5 Jul 27	6/7 Continued		Two bicycles lost in 16%, in charge of No. 3/Cy written off	M.P
	7/7		No. T/3/026059 D. WHYTE J. reported from R. in 6th mnt. posted to H. & Cy. No. T/24031 A/Cpl FINSON B.J. died in No. 36 C.C.S. in 6th mnt.	M.P
	8/7		No. T/ 9333 A/L/Cpl MAHER No. 1 Cy. transferred to H. & Cy. in Kinder No. No. in charge No. 2 Cy. evacuated.	M.P
	9/7		2nd Lt. A. HARRISON A.S.C. joined from 52nd Divisional Train. No. T/261527 D. MAIR R. joined from 52nd D.T.	M.P
	10/7		No. M2/098462 Pte TAYLOR b. posted from 41st M.T.Cy. in 9th mnt. vice No. M2/079874 Pte FENWICK J.H. evacuated 8 mnt. De 1129. Lost No. 97 in charge No. 1 Cy. killed by shell fire evacuated. -123-	M.P
	11/7		No. T/ 8697 S/Sgt. ARTHUR No. 4 Cy. evacuated to 2nd Canadian C.C.S. 28%	M.P
	12/7		8 Drivers awarded 1st G.C. Badge	M.P

WAR DIARY
INTELLIGENCE SUMMARY

Army Form C. 2118.

Place	Date	Hour	Summary of Events and Information	Remarks and references to Appendices
K.21.6.6.5 Sheet 27	12/7/18	Continued	S.A.G.M. No. T³/023752 W. T. TATE, No. 1 (G) was tried by S.A.G.M. on 9th inst. on the following charge:— "Disobeying a lawful command given by his superior officer i.e. Refusal to given his horse jiler wheel to do so by Captain T. Banks MILNE R.F.A." The accused was found guilty & sentenced to undergo 42 days F.P. No. 1.	M.P.
	13/7/18		Captain E. H. TRUTER A.S.C. invalided to England 29/6/18. No. T⁴/042927 W SWALES W. ho. + (G) invalided 28/6/18.	M.P.
	14/7/18		One G.S. wagon No. E. 137676 received from DEPOT. 10⁴ Divn. for use 41.² Batt. M.G. Corps. Supplies.	M.P.
	15/7/18		One mule No. 10 in charge No. 1 (G) evacuated.	M.P.

WAR DIARY
INTELLIGENCE SUMMARY
(Erase heading not required.)

Army Form C. 2118.

Place	Date	Hour	Summary of Events and Information	Remarks and references to Appendices
K.21.b.q.r Sheet 21.	16/7/18		Usual routine	M.P.
	17/7/18		Driver No. 6693 rejoined from S.A.D.O.S.	M.P.
	18/7/18		Captain E.S. NEEDHAM A.S.C. (T.F.) joined from No. 31 Railhead Supply Detachment. Posted to No. 4 Coy as Supply Officer 124th Inf. Bde. No. 2 Coy move to K.26.d.7.9. Sheet 27.	M.P.
	19/7/18		Usual routine. Dvr R.L.D. No. 62 in charge of No. 2 Coy evacuated	M.P.
	20/7/18		No. T/040835 Sjt Low C. joined from Base Depot.	M.P.
	21/7/18		Usual routine	M.P.
	22/7/18		No. T/058905 D. ANDREWS G.F. No. 1 Coy evacuated	M.P.
	23/7/18		No. T/36792 a/S/Sgt KIRK J. No. 4 Coy reverts to Pte. Coy 9. of Spoon in admin to Pte. 26 Coy	M.P.

WAR DIARY
or
INTELLIGENCE SUMMARY.
(Erase heading not required.)

Army Form C. 2118.

Place	Date	Hour	Summary of Events and Information	Remarks and references to Appendices
K.21. b & c Sheet 27	24/7/18		Normal routine	M.R.
	25/7/18		15ᵗʰ Reinforcement join from Base Depot.	M.R.
	26/7/18		No. T/14568 Sgt. (RSM) DUGGAN. H.J Promoted L/Sgt. R.R. 19/7/18. No. T/7266 L/Cpl (Sdn.S.Sgt) STURGESS A.C. promoted A/L/Sgt. 18/7/18. No. T24017 Dr (A/Sgt) BEACH J. appointed A/Cpl. 26/7/18. Authority A.T.6. order 43 of 3/7/18.	M.R.
	27/7/18		Capt. W.S. MAUE rejoined from R.	M.R.
	28/7/18		No. S/864536 Pte GRIFFITHS B.R. (Clerk) joined from 39 & Div. Train.	M.R.
	29/7/18		Normal routine	M.R.
	30/7/18		No. T/275.0735 Dr NEWBOLD F. No.2 (4) transferred to 738 tol. Amrit. No. T/56762 Cpl ELLARD H.J. joined from Base Depot. No. T/364631 Pte CLAYDON A.F. joined from 39 & Div. Train.	M.R.
	31/7/18		Normal routine	M.R.

M. Hoole Captain
In Command, 41ˢᵗ Divisional Train

WAR DIARY
or
INTELLIGENCE SUMMARY.
(Erase heading not required.)

Army Form C. 2118.

Place	Date	Hour	Summary of Events and Information	Remarks and references to Appendices
K21.b.8.5. Steenwerck 27.	1/8.		Usual routine. No. T/279153 Dr WRIGHT W. No. 4 Coy returned to Base S.I.P. for indemnification by S. Melbourne.	M.P.
	2/8		Usual routine.	M.P.
	3/8.		No. T/14565 B.S.M. DUGGAN H.J. attached to 26th Bn. R. Fusiliers for 1 month pending the taking up of a temporary commission.	M.P.
	4/8.		No. T/045379 A/L/Cpl FARBROTHER W.T. } Anglure to Establishment Pte CLAYDON A.F. } Rets to Base Depot. Pte STINTON A. }	M.P.
	5/8		S/465125 S.Q.M.S. TAYLOR W.R. Promoted W.O. cl. 2. Auth A.O. 194 - 1918. T/264690 Dr PARNELL W. No. 1 Coy vacated 27/8. T/407726 Pte HEMS R. from No. 1 Coy to No. 3 Coy. T/31792 Dr KIRK J. No. 4 Coy apptd A/Cpl w.l.p.a Auth: ASC P32/14416/L cy 3/8/18	M.P.
	6/8.		Ord. J.L.O. No. 119 in charge No. 2 Coy vacated 5th inst.	M.P.

Army Form C. 2118.

WAR DIARY
or
INTELLIGENCE SUMMARY.
(Erase heading not required.)

Instructions regarding War Diaries and Intelligence Summaries are contained in F. S. Regs., Part II. and the Staff Manual respectively. Title pages will be prepared in manuscript.

Place	Date	Hour	Summary of Events and Information	Remarks and references to Appendices
K.21.6.6.5.	7/8/18		Usual routine.	M.P
Area 27	8/8/18		No. S/314096 Pte EVANS T.H. awarded 28 days F.P. No.1 for overstaying his leave to the United Kingdom	M.P
	9/8/18		Usual routine.	M.P
	10/8/18		21 Category "B" driver join to replace "A" men. No. T/9149 A/L/Cpl PATRICK C.E. joined from Base Depot.	M.P
	11/8/18		3 Category "B" driver join to replace "A" men. 5 Men awarded 1st G.C. Badge.	M.P
	12/8/18		25 Category "A" driver returned to A.S.C. Base Depot. T/101580 Dr FRASER D. No.1 Coy evacuated 11/8/18. 1 Rider No. 12. on charge No.1 Coy evacuated 9th inst	M.P
	13/8/18		T/370493 Dr PERRY S.W. Category "B" joined to complete 25 T/132533 Sgt NUNES J. evacuated to 2nd Canadian C.C.S.	M.P

WAR DIARY
or
INTELLIGENCE SUMMARY.
(Erase heading not required.)

Army Form C. 2118.

Place	Date	Hour	Summary of Events and Information	Remarks and references to Appendices
K.21.6.8.5. SHEET. 27	14/8/18		Tm/2H2660 Dr. PLOWDEN V.A.I.B. No 3. Coy transferred to No 1 Coy 1 H/g No 151. on Charge No 1 Coy, Air hose Ink ind	M.P.
	15/8/18		Usual routine	M.P.
	16 "		Tm/045078 Cpl. CATLIN Ch. No 2 Coy } Qualified as GAS NCOs Tm/060725. Cpl. SANDERSON. J.H. No 1 Coy	M.P.
	17 "		Usual routine	M.P.
	18 "		6 A.D. weewos from Remounts on 17th ind	M.P.
	19 "		No T2/9655 Dr. PETY W. No 2 Coy transferred to 138th. Field Amb:	M.P.
	20 "		One Mule No 9 on Charge No 1 Coy evacuated.	M.P.
	21 "		No Tm/123744 L/Sergt. SCOTT. J.E. No 2 Coy promoted Sergt Authority :- QSC Sect. 937/15390 Ad/20 8/18	M.P.
	22 "		Gas Course. {Tm/211754 Cpl. JENNY. B.M. No 1 Coy Failed T3/026988. Cpl. PANT. F.W. 3.1 Passed.	M.P.
	23 "		One Mule received from Remounts on 22nd ind	M.P.
	24.		One H.D. No 150 on Charge No 1 Coy evacuated	M.P.

WAR DIARY
or
INTELLIGENCE SUMMARY.
(Erase heading not required.)

Army Form C. 2118.

Place	Date	Hour	Summary of Events and Information	Remarks and references to Appendices
K.21.6.8.5. Sheet: 27	25/8/18		S/294998. Pte. PRESTON H. No 2 Coy. Retd to ASC Base Depot So duty as Clerk. TS/9333. S/dt Cpl. MAHER P No 1 Coy " " " " Surplus to Establishment	M.P.
	26."		S/355635. Pte CARPENTER MA THQrs transferred to No 2 Coy	M.P.
	27.		Routine as usual.	M.P.
	28/8.		No. T/233350 D/Pickering S. No 3 Coy transferred to 29 Div Train. No. 2 Coy moved to HALLINES	M.P.
	29/8.		I am Pvt Ok Moved to WIZERNES No. 3 Coy moved to ST. MARTIN AU LAERT staying night 29/30 at RENESCURE.	M.P.
WIZERNES FRANCE	30/8.		Usual routine. No. T/324 242 Sgt. HARWOOD W.J. joined from 31 Div. Train 29".	M.P.
	31/8.		Usual routine	M.P.

M. Ock Captain
Commdg. 41st Div. Train.

Army Form C. 2118.

WAR DIARY
or
INTELLIGENCE SUMMARY.
(Erase heading not required.)

Vol 29

Place	Date	Hour	Summary of Events and Information	Remarks and references to Appendices
WIZERNES FRANCE	1/9/18		Capt. E.M WOOF. A.S.C. admitted 102nd F.Amb. (sick) via R.I.A 5.8. Shel 27. No.1 Coy move to	MG
	2/8		No.1 Coy move to L.33 d 3.3. Shel 27. No.2 & 3 Coys move Park to AIRELLE Aren J.H.Q. Transport move to AIRELLE Aren 2nd Lt J. CAVANAGH. A.S.S. admitted to 2nd F.Amb. (sick) n Park	MG
K.24.a.9.8 Shel 27	3/9/18		2am HdQr move to K.24.a.7.6. Shel 27. No.1 Coy move to R.I. a.7.9. Shel 27.	MG
	4/9/18		Capt. E.M WOOF A.S.C discharged from P. No. T3. 017266 Sgt PATTERSON J. joined from Base Depot + retransferred 139 F. Amb.	MG
	5/9/18		No. T.394472 D. NELSON S.B. No.2 Coy invalided on 25/8/18. 3 Ridden + 1 Pack received from Remounts.	MG
	6/9/18		One H.D. Lno.118' in charge No.2 Coy died 2/9/18.	MG

Army Form C. 2118.

WAR DIARY
or
INTELLIGENCE SUMMARY.
(Erase heading not required.)

Place	Date	Hour	Summary of Events and Information	Remarks and references to Appendices
K.24.a.6.1 Sheet 27	7/7/18		No. T/26301 2/Lorimer F. No 1 Coy. reverted 21/8. No. 1 Coy moves to L.17.c.2.8. Sheet 27. No. 2 " " L.28.d.3.7. " No. 3 " Coy " L.23.c.3.4 "	MP
	8/7/18		Promotion. No. T/211386 2/Cpl. Mortimer S.F. 131st Fd Amb. Promoted Cpl. 28/8/17. No. T/3/027083 A/Cpl. Gibbs W.H. No.1 Coy Promoted Cpl. 7/7/18. No. T/4/238673 A/A/Cpl. Luff S.P. No.1 Coy " A/Cpl. 23/7/18. " 064816 A/Cpl. Jarvis R.B. No. 3 Coy Cpl. 27/5/18. Th. S+G " " Cpl. 6/7/18 Authority No. A.S.C. P. no/16146 of 6/7/18.	MP
	9/7/18		Usual routine.	MP

WAR DIARY
or
INTELLIGENCE SUMMARY.
(Erase heading not required.)

Army Form C. 2118.

Instructions regarding War Diaries and Intelligence Summaries are contained in F. S. Regs., Part II. and the Staff Manual respectively. Title pages will be prepared in manuscript.

Place	Date	Hour	Summary of Events and Information	Remarks and references to Appendices
K24.a.9.8. Ser 21.	10/4/18		2 Frank awarded 1st G.C. Badge. No. T4/248315 Pte Callaghan W returned 1st G.C. Badge 7/4.	MP
	11/4/18		2nd Lieut. J. Cavanagh A.S.C. returned to duty from R.	MP
	12/4/18		Usual routine.	MP
	13/4/18		Usual routine.	MP
	14/4/18		No. 4 Coy move to work for Licques Area.	MP
	15/4/18		No. T4/250123 Cpl Storey E, promotion of to rank of Corporal antedated to 2nd April 1918. Authority No. A.S.C. P.37/15441/28 of 12/4/18. No. 4 Coy at Clerques.	MP
	16/4/18		No. T/14568 T.S.S.M. Duggan H J No. 1 Coy proceeded to England 15th inst for admittance to a Cadet School. Struck off No. T4/043270 Pte McHugh R. No. 1 Coy awarded 28 days F.P. No 1. for overstaying his leave to the U.K.	MP

WAR DIARY
or
INTELLIGENCE SUMMARY.
(Erase heading not required.)

Army Form C. 2118.

Instructions regarding War Diaries and Intelligence Summaries are contained in F.S. Regs., Part II. and the Staff Manual respectively. Title pages will be prepared in manuscript.

Place	Date	Hour	Summary of Events and Information	Remarks and references to Appendices
K.24.a.9.5. Shed 27.	17/9/18		No. 3 Coy moved to Shed 27. L. 33. entd. T/ 042415 N Withers A.S. from H.Q. to No. 1 Coy. T/242660 N Plowden V No. 1 Coy to Siege H.Q.	WP
	18/9/18		No. T/390600 N Cooper E joined from 20 L Div Train. T/381041 N Oakley, A.H. No. 3 Coy transferred 18 Bun. One H.Q. horse No. 88 in charge of No. 1 Coy transferred 17 Bun.	WP
	19/9/18		No. 1 Coy moved to L. 34. c. 4. 6. Shed 27.	WP
	20/9/18		No. T/044653 Qr. S.M. Mulcahy C.F. No. 4 Coy promoted C.S.M. with effect from 21/3/18. Auth. Casc. P. 235/14819 of 16/9/18 No. T/144251 N Bagshaw W.F. placed on 1st rate of Cps. Pay from 1st September 1918.	WP
	21/9/18		No. T/030861 A/Cpl Carlyle A.D. joined from Base Depot. T/712 N Button F. do do T/361333 Mears W. do do	WP

A 5834 Wt. W4973/M687 750,000 8/16 D. D. & L. Ltd. Forms/C2118/13

Army Form C. 2118.

WAR DIARY
or
INTELLIGENCE SUMMARY.
(Erase heading not required.)

Place	Date	Hour	Summary of Events and Information	Remarks and references to Appendices
K.24.a.9.1	20/9/18	Cont.	2nd Lieut. R.W. MAYSON. A.S.C. joined from A.S.C. Base Depot. No. T/3/026755 D ELBECK. T. awarded 14 days F.P. No 2. August 96 daily 10/9/18	M.P. M.P.
Sheet 27	21/9/18		The M.O. Lieut No. S.6 in charge No. 1 (Q) transferred 20/9/18.	M.P.
	22/9/18		The Corporal SKS Lieut transferred from No. 3 (Q) to No. 1 (Q)	M.P.
	23/9/18		2nd Lt. A.W. ROULSTON. A.S.C. proceeded to report to O.C. Base Supply Depot. ROUEN. (Revert of strength)	M.P.
	24/9/18		No. T/235830 D HALL. S. joined from No. 7 Army Aux. Horse Co.	M.P.
	25/9/18		No. T/4/275533 N. PARRY. S. No. 3 (Q) transferred to No. 10. G.S. 22 9/18	M.P.
	26/9/18		No. 4 (Q) move from CLERAVES to work for the area. No. S/SR. 1152 Pte. PICKLES J.A. transferred to No. 62 C.C.S. ~ 23/9/18. No. T4/215727 D DOCKMANTON. S.J. transferred to 140 P.A. Coyk.	M.P. M.P.

WAR DIARY
or
INTELLIGENCE SUMMARY.
(Erase heading not required.)

Army Form C. 2118.

Place	Date	Hour	Summary of Events and Information	Remarks and references to Appendices
K.24.a.9.6. Sheet 27.	27/8		Area Headquarters move to DALLINGTON CAMP Sheet 27/2.29.c.8.2. No 4 Coy move at do On Rates No 77 inchange No 2 recruited. No 1057257 D. MILLER J. No 2 (D) app accept from 26/8 and rank Pay from 28/8 vice No. 536792 a/Sgt. KIRK J admitted @ 26/8 Cont. OS P/t 3/167974 J 2573/16.	M.O.
DALLINGTON CAMP Sheet 27 2.29.c.f.2.	28/8		On H.Q. No 39 re large No 1 (D) recruited. Area Headquarters move to DOMINION CAMP Sheet 28 N.W. G.23.6.5.4. No 1 (Coy) move to Sheet 28/ G.12.a.7.3. 2 " " " Sheet 28/ G.11.a. central 3 " " " " G.11.c.5.6. 4 " " " " G.11.c.5.6.	M.O.
DOMINION CAMP Sheet 28 G.23.b.8.4.	29/8		On H.Q. No. 22 re large No. 2 (D) recruited.	M.O.

Army Form C. 2118.

WAR DIARY
or
INTELLIGENCE SUMMARY.
(Erase heading not required.)

Place	Date	Hour	Summary of Events and Information	Remarks and references to Appendices
Dominion Camp Shed 26. G.23. C.f.4.	30/1		Gravillin — The undermentioned were wounded on the night 28th/29th by bomb dropped by hostile aircraft. T/057709 Corpl FISHER T T/057996 Driv DICKENS A	N.P

M. Potter Captain
Commanding 41st Divisional Train

WAR DIARY
or
INTELLIGENCE SUMMARY.

Army Form C. 2118.

Vol 30

Place	Date	Hour	Summary of Events and Information	Remarks and references to Appendices
DOMINION CAMP Sheet 28 G.23.b.5.4.	1/9/18		No. 1 Coy. move to Sheet 28/ H.36.b.6.5. 2 " " H.36.b.f.3 3 " " H.24.c.3.4 4 " " H.30.a.5.9.	N/F
	2/9/18		T/76762 Cpl Ellard H.T. promoted Corporal from 16/7/18 (Authority) T/1316 a/Cpl Brown appointed L/Cpl 7/8/18 ACI. P20/16.4.18 & 26/16) T/066886 " Kent A.T. " 6/7/18	N/F
	3/9/18		One G.S. wagon in charge of No. 1 Coy fell into shell hole on night 1st and 2nd covering the movement.	N/F
	4/9/18		H.Q. & Train H.Q. 1st move to Sheet 28/ I.26.c.o.1 No. 1 Coy. do H.18.c.3.4 2 " do H.24.c.3.2 3 " do H.24.c.3.2 4 " do H.24.c.3.2	N/F

Army Form C. 2118.

WAR DIARY
or
INTELLIGENCE SUMMARY.
(Erase heading not required.)

Instructions regarding War Diaries and Intelligence Summaries are contained in F. S. Regs., Part II. and the Staff Manual respectively. Title pages will be prepared in manuscript.

Place	Date	Hour	Summary of Events and Information	Remarks and references to Appendices
LANKHOF CAMP Sheet 28. I 26. c. o. 1	5/12		Corpl. E.S. NEEDHAM O/S admitted (sick) to Fld Ambulance (Station of 2nd NZ Div) in 3rd Field	M.P.
	6/12		One N.C.O. Horse in charge No. 1 Coy wounded by bomb on night 28/29th Sept. One Rider attd 3 Coy (awaiting posting) killed by bomb on night 28/29 Sept. No. 130670 Dr POTTER A. No. 4 Coy evacuated N.Z. Stat. D. 2nd Field.	M.P.
	6/12		No. 2 Coy moved to Sheet 28/G.19.c.9.c. One Rider received from Remounts & Stores.	M.P.
	7/12		No. 4 Coy moved to Sheet 27/L.17.c.2.8.	M.P.
	8/12		An O.R.'s ways received from Stores.	M.P.
	9/12		Mount routine	M.P.
	10/12		2 O/Ranks awarded 1st G.C. Badge	M.P.
	11/12		One N.C.O Horse No. 1 Coy + Horse No. 1 Coy evacuated. No. 4 Coy moved to Sheet 27/L.21.d.5.7.	M.P.

Army Form C. 2118.

WAR DIARY
or
INTELLIGENCE SUMMARY.
(Erase heading not required.)

Instructions regarding War Diaries and Intelligence Summaries are contained in F. S. Regs., Part II. and the Staff Manual respectively. Title pages will be prepared in manuscript.

Place	Date	Hour	Summary of Events and Information	Remarks and references to Appendices
LANKHOF CAMP Sheet 28 I.26.c.0.1	12/10/18		Saw M.O. have in charge No 3 Coy dismounted 11 hour	[sig]
	13/10/18		No. 1 Coy move to WOODCOTE HOUSE Sheet 28/ I.20.c.t.3. No. 4 " " " SWAN CHATEAU	[sig]
	14/10/18		No. 3 Coy move to Sheet 28/ I.9.c. central. 4 Reinforcements for from Base Depot.	[sig]
	15/10/18		No. 747/22207 Cpl. KENDALL S.H. joined from 34 C.Ox. Train	[sig]
	16/10/18		Gun Headquarters move to DADIZEELE Sheet 28/ K.12.c.2.1. No. 1 Coy move to Sheet 28/ K.24.a.3.9. " 2 " " " K.17.d.9.9. " 3 " " " K.17.b.9.1. " 4 " " " K.17.c.0.1.	[sig]
DADIZEELE Sheet 28 K.12.c.2.1.	17/10/18		Cleans routine.	[sig]

Army Form C. 2118.

WAR DIARY
or
INTELLIGENCE SUMMARY.
(Erase heading not required.)

Instructions regarding War Diaries and Intelligence Summaries are contained in F. S. Regs., Part II. and the Staff Manual respectively. Title pages will be prepared in manuscript.

Place	Date	Hour	Summary of Events and Information	Remarks and references to Appendices
DADIZEELE Sheet 28. K.12.c.2.	16/10		3 N.O.R. have in charge No. 1 Eq. wounded 12 E.M. wounded 1 " " " " " 4 " "	M
	19/10		Nowt worked.	M
	20/10		Lain Hd-Qtr. mov to Sheet 29. G.14.c.6.3 on the MOORSEELE—CULLEGHEM Road. No. 1 Eq. mov to Sheet 29/ G.19.d.6.9. " 2 " " " G. 25. b.9.9. " 3 " " " G. 25. b.9.9. " 4 " " Sheet 28/ L. 24. c.4.7.	M
	21/10		Lain Hd-Qtr mov to BISSEGHEM Sheet 29. G.36.a.2.7. No. 1 Eq mov to Sheet 29. b.4.2 " 2 " " " G. 29. c. 6.3. " 3 " " " G. 29. b. 4.2 " 4 " " G. 29. b.4.2	M
BISSEGHEM Sheet 29. G. 36.a.2.7.	22/10		Shot N.O.R. have received from Remounts	M

WAR DIARY
or
INTELLIGENCE SUMMARY.
(Erase heading not required.)

Army Form C. 2118.

Place	Date	Hour	Summary of Events and Information	Remarks and references to Appendices
BISSEGHEM Map 29 G.36.a.2.7.	23/9/18		No. T/SP/01652 Dr (A/Cpl) POSKITT. W joined from Bnc Depot. No. T/4/065292 Dr ROSIER A evacuated C.C.S. 19 End 1 Ridn No. 13 . 1 M.D. No. 65 on large No. (G) remounted 10 & 17 Inm.	M.P
	24/9/18		An H.Q. horse received from Remount 22 End	M.P
	25/9/18		T/3/029912 Sal/M/S MILLS. W. No. 1 (G) remounted 21 End T/4/23600M Dr PEARSON J.H. No. 4 G - do - 23 End	M.P
	26/9/18		Two H.D. v1 Ridn received from Remount.	M.P
	27/9/18		No T/3/027702 Dr HUNTER R. No. 2 (G) awarded 28 days F.P. No. 1 by F.G.C.M. for GC Boutyes 27/9 for overstaying his leave.	M.P
	28/9/18		No. T/4/260513 Dr WILKINSON R. No. 1 (G) transferred to 52nd M.V.S. T/4/094188 Dr WATKINS S.J. joined from 52nd M.V.S.	M.P

Army Form C. 2118.

WAR DIARY
or
INTELLIGENCE SUMMARY.
(Erase heading not required.)

Place	Date	Hour	Summary of Events and Information	Remarks and references to Appendices
BISSEGHEM sheet 29 G.36.a.27	29/10/18		Army HQ. moved to COURTRAI sheet 29 N.2.6.3.8. No. 1 Coy " " H. 32.b.2.3 " 2 " " H. 33.c.1.2 " 3 " " H. 32.b.1.2 " 4 " " H. 32.d.4.3 " 5 location from 235th Emp. Coy. 28/10/18 " 6 Reinforcements from from R.E. Base Depot.	MP
COURTRAI sheet 29 N.2.6.3.8.	30/10/18		T/302402 Cpl. HARWOOD J.W. No. 1 Coy. Evacuated 27/10 H/344153 Drvr. PRIME B. No. 3 Coy. " 27/10	MP
	31/10/18		No. T/SR. 07552 A/Cpl. POSKITT. W. To " G" Tunnellers. to 4th Army Area. Have company this Auth: of D.A.G. "2nd Army" Serial No. R.899 of 27/1/918.	MP

M Poole Capt RE
Commdg. N° 2 Coy Trmp

WAR DIARY
INTELLIGENCE SUMMARY.
(Erase heading not required.)

Army Form C. 2118.

41 D Train Vol 31

Place	Date	Hour	Summary of Events and Information	Remarks and references to Appendices
COURTRAI Sheet 29/N2.6.30.1½	1/11/18		To H.W.F.N.3 D. Butler C.A. No. 1 @ recovated 29/½ Re N.D. No 58 in charge No. 1 @ vacated	WM
	2/11/18		Div M.G. Offr moved to SWEVEGHEM Sheet 29/ O.1.a.6.5. No. 1 @ moved to H.34.c.8.4 „ 2 „ „ „ „ N.6.a.37 „ 3 „ „ „ „ H.34.c.6.5 „ 4 „ „ „ „ N.6.6.5.1.	WM
SWEVEGHEM Sheet 29/O.1.a.6.5	3/11/18		Captain H.W.W. Nixon 2nd Lt R.A. Major admitted 140th Fd Amb (sick) To S.46/536 Pte Griffiths left the "G" recovated 66.S. 17½	WM
	4/11/18		Lieut P.B. Embry admitted 140th Fd Amb (sick) On Bd Loss 47 m Lays to 2 Lys No.1 @ moved to Sheet 29/ I 25 central „ 2 „ „ „ „ I 26.d.3.7 Capt W.B. Pollard reported to Employment Bureau Regt to report to General Direct of Medical appointment for transfer to R.of W. Co.	WM

Army Form C. 2118.

WAR DIARY
or
INTELLIGENCE SUMMARY.
(Erase heading not required.)

Instructions regarding War Diaries and Intelligence Summaries are contained in F. S. Regs., Part II. and the Staff Manual respectively. Title pages will be prepared in manuscript.

Place	Date	Hour	Summary of Events and Information	Remarks and references to Appendices
SWEVEGHEM Sheet 29/I.21 b.65	5/11		Our Headquarters move to Sheet 29/I.32.b.11 ESSCHER	
			No 3 Coy "	
			No 4 " "	
			" " I.33.a.6.6.	20th
ESSCHER Sheet 29/I.32.b.11	6/11		Captain H. Morris returned to duty from R. to 3rd Bgd	
			No. 0/5.7370 D. YOUNG J.R. No 2 Coy awarded 1st clasp F.P. No. 1	
			Badge 6/11 for neglecting his leave to the U.K.	20th
	7/11		Our Headquarters move to Sheet 29/I.9.b.7.3 SNEPHOEK to DEERLYCK	
			No 1 Coy move to I.3.d.2.3	
			" 2 " " I.3.b.3.6	
			" 3 " " I.9.a.5.1	
			" 4 " " I.9.b.4.5.	20th
SNEPHOEK 8/11	8/11		No T/15515 Sgt VOSPER G.S. promoted on mark towar in re-engagement (L/R-S-M)	
Sheet 29/I.9.b.7.3	9/11		No T/03962 S/S/Sgt Mills W. returned from Base Depot.	
			T/042788 N Gray R. + T/17033 N Ball E. succeeded L/C.S.M.'s	
			T/35651 N APPLEGEE H. No 3 Coy transferred HQ. 123 Coy Royal Kent	20th

Army Form C2118/15.

Army Form C. 2118.

WAR DIARY
INTELLIGENCE SUMMARY.
(Erase heading not required.)

Instructions regarding War Diaries and Intelligence Summaries are contained in F. S. Regs., Part II. and the Staff Manual respectively. Title pages will be prepared in manuscript.

Place	Date	Hour	Summary of Events and Information	Remarks and references to Appendices
INGOYHEM Sheet 29/J.7.d.9.1	10/11		Div. Headquarters moved to Sheet 29/J.27.d.9.1	
			No. 1 Coy — do — J.34.a.3.1	
			2 — do — J.34.a.3.6	
			3 — do — J.33.a.9.0	
			4 — do — J.33.d.0.9	
	11/11		2 Lieut. awarded M.C. (Badge)	Wills
			Coys Headquarters move to Sheet 30/M.14.d.9.1 KERKHEM	
			No. 1 (9)	
			2 " 29.Q.21.6.6.4.	
			3 " 30.M.20.6.1.3.	
			4 "	
KERKHEM Sheet 30 M.14. d.9.1	12/11		No. F/17543 a/L/M. YORK C.H. struck off strength. A.L.6 P.461/1734/16 dd 2/11.	Wills
			No. T/24017 Sgt. BEACH.J. No. 1 Coy app. O/C S.M — vice a/M. a/2	
			No. T/060725 Cpl. SANDERSON J.H. No.1 Coy. app. a/Sgt.	
			No. T/094214 L/Cpl. COX H. No.1 Coy. app. a/Cpl.	
			No. T/065871 Pte. BARRY J.W. No.1 Coy. app. a/L/Cpl.	
			No. F/24017 S/C.S.M. BEACH J. transferred to 140th Fd. Amb. and struck off strength. A/E P461/1734/16 dd 3/11/16	E.W.M

WAR DIARY
INTELLIGENCE SUMMARY

Army Form C. 2118.

Place	Date	Hour	Summary of Events and Information	Remarks and references to Appendices
KERKHEM Sheet 20 M11 d 9.4	13/11		Transfer. Pte F.15513 D.O.M. Perry A.R. No 3 Cy to No 1 Cy. F.17543 do York C.H.	WWh
			Lieut. B.A. Emby R.S.C. returned to duty from R. on 10th inst.	
	14/11		Bar. Hd qrs moved to Shet 30 N.17. d. 7.5 / N.17 a.1.9 / N.23 a.9.9 / N.17 c.5.4.	Wth
			No 1 Cy mnd to Shet 30 N.17.d.7.5	
			" 2 " N.17.a.1.9	
			" 3 " N.23.a.9.9	
			" 4 " N.17.c.5.4	
	15/11		No. T.2/3926 L/c Matthews J. No 4 Cy died on 12 inst in No 5 t General D from Pneumonia. Buried on 13th inst in TERLINCTHUN Military Cemetery. Grave No. 10 E Plot 9.	
			No 54/072284 Cpl. Ashworth J. 2nd A/Cpl. awarded 13 Bar	
			Transfer No. TR/237472 L/Cpl Scott W.R. No 4 Cy to No 1 Cy / TR/211754 L/Cpl Denny B.N. No 1 Cy to No 4 / 072284 Cpl Kirk J. No 4 Cy to No 1 Cy	

Army Form C. 2118.

WAR DIARY
INTELLIGENCE SUMMARY.
(Erase heading not required.)

Instructions regarding War Diaries and Intelligence Summaries are contained in F. S. Regs., Part II. and the Staff Manual respectively. Title pages will be prepared in manuscript.

Place	Date	Hour	Summary of Events and Information	Remarks and references to Appendices
NEDERBRAKEL Sheet 30 N.17.	16th		A.6. (T.F.) Captain T. FLEMING. MC. OBE reported to the battalion & took over A.6 (T.F.) Records 14 1918. (ordered from London Gazette of 14/4/18).	
	17th		One H.Q. No.129 in charge Mr L.G. transferred. 1st Front line from 238th Emp Coy on loan. 1st H.Q. Lorries received from Kempnete.	W.M.
	18th		The moved to the GERMAN Front commencing Army Headquarters now to SANTBERGEN Sheet 30/Q.15. No. 1 Coy move to LUST Sheet 30 Q.14. 2 " VIANE 27 V.24. 3 " GAMMERAGES W.15. 4 " MEERSCHWBORG Q.24.	W.M.

Army Form C. 2118.

WAR DIARY
INTELLIGENCE SUMMARY.
(Erase heading not required.)

Place	Date	Hour	Summary of Events and Information	Remarks and references to Appendices
SANTBERGEN				
Oct 3/9.18	19th		3 M.D. Lorries Nos. 49, 52(53) in charge of No. 1 Coy dismantled on 14 Sept 15 2nd	with
	20th		No. 2 Coy moved EVERBECQ Hd. Qrs of U.S.A.H.H.	
			" 3 " " LES DEUX ACREN.	
			" 4 " " VIANE	with
	21st		Army Headquarters move to 27 Almeridend, GRAMMONT.	with
GRAMMONT	22nd		No. M/09074 Pte. BALDWIN. A. v Irwham convey of M.T.M.T.	with
Oct 3.			No. M/25614 52 Pte. TAYLOR C. v Irwham car No. 17719 left 20.18
V. 2.			Cadet Duncan Sloans
	23rd		4 Driver join from Base Depot.	with

WAR DIARY
INTELLIGENCE SUMMARY

Army Form C. 2118.

Place	Date	Hour	Summary of Events and Information	Remarks and references to Appendices
GRAMMONT del 9 N.2.	24/11		Promotions - Sergeant A/ S.J.W	
			H/5617 a/Cpl. SCARRATT F. Promoted T/Sgt. with effect from 27/11	
			H/20336 A/L/Sgt. PULLEN H. " T/Sgt.	
			H/17206 A/L/Sgt. STURGESS W.C. " T/Sgt.	6/7/12/17
			H/6471 A/Sgt. CLARKSON J. " T/Sgt.	24/7
			H/20052 A/Sgt. STIRRUP J. " T/Sgt.	3/16
			H/10511 A/Sgt. VESPER G.S. " T/Sgt.	4/16
			H/22534 A/Cpl. GRIDLEY H. " T/Cpl.	3/16
			H/26973 A/Cpl. SMITH G " T/Cpl.	23/17
			H/27125 A/L/Cpl. CARROLL J.F.S. " T/L/Cpl.	3/15
			H/36142 A/L/Cpl. KING J " A/Cpl.	28/7
			H/36147 A/L/Cpl. SMITH J.E. " A/Cpl.	20/7
				9/16
			Coll. Addl. Prs. P.D.1/4/21 + 4 8.3	
	25/11		Two J.O. Levee received from Remount 24/11.	20/11
	26/11		No. 74/25991 Pte. BRYANT A. Thos.	20/11
			74/062263 " CULPIN R " } Evacuated to 6.6.J.	
			74/364140 " COX J " } 28/11	
			-2	
			-3	28/11

Army Form C. 2118.

WAR DIARY
or
INTELLIGENCE SUMMARY.
(Erase heading not required.)

Instructions regarding War Diaries and Intelligence Summaries are contained in F. S. Regs., Part II. and the Staff Manual respectively. Title pages will be prepared in manuscript.

Place	Date	Hour	Summary of Events and Information	Remarks and references to Appendices
GRAMMONT Sheet 30 v 2.	27th		336239 A/ WILLIAMS C.W. No 2 Cy transferred to 122nd Inf. Bde. this day. T/23419 — HILTON E. & 122 B/Maff. rejoined this day on posting to No. 2 Cy	W/M
			H.O. Lce. No. 32 on extended ly 52nd M.V.S. in 25. - dog.s - posted to Div 'G'	W/M
	28th		No T/235830 A/ Hall S. awarded 14 days F.P. No.1. n 26% for underlying his issue to the U.K.	W/M
	29th		C.O. inspect: 1st Line transport of 122nd Inf. Bde H.O. Lorries in charge No 39 December 25th	W/M
	30th		No. I/10027 A/C.S.M. FLOWER S.H. join'd fm. No 929 Cy. H.S.C. + transferred to 131st 4th Corps	W/M

W Ss Wade
Commdg H.Q. Coy.
G Team

WAR DIARY
or
INTELLIGENCE SUMMARY.
(Erase heading not required.)

Army Form C. 2118.

Place	Date	Hour	Summary of Events and Information	Remarks and references to Appendices
GRAMMONT Sheet 30 V.2	1/8/18		No. T/10027 A/S/M Flower S.H. appointed A.S/M n. Trumps to 131 T.A.	
	2/8/18		No. T/36973 Cpl. Smith G. To "G" app. A/Sgt. 27/7 until pay from 3/7 T/026856 A/Cpl. Kent A.T. To 3 G " A/Cpl 2/7 " 3/7 T/062390 Dr. Wass C. To 1 G " A/Cpl 2/7 " 3/7 Auth: A.6 CR51/18052/9 4/27/7 A.A.D. No 187 n. charge M. 3 G reminder	
	3/7/18		T/124-953 A/L/Cpl Walker S.G. S/355835 Pte. Carpenter M.A. T/035221 " Goodliffe A. ⎫ T/23951 " McCaul R. ⎬ Reminder G.G.S. T/5303 A/M. Nunn A.C. ⎭ 28/7 + 29/7	
	4/8/18		2nd Lieut. R.W. Mayson retired to duty from R.	
	5/8/18		T/026957 Dr. Davison R.G. proceed to Base Depot for transfer to England on compassionate grounds. Auth: D.A.G. No CR/11773/A of 2/8/16	

Army Form C. 2118.

WAR DIARY
or
INTELLIGENCE SUMMARY.
(Erase heading not required.)

Instructions regarding War Diaries and Intelligence Summaries are contained in F. S. Regs., Part II. and the Staff Manual respectively. Title pages will be prepared in manuscript.

Place	Date	Hour	Summary of Events and Information	Remarks and references to Appendices
GRAMMENT	6/2/18		No. T/3/023359 N. HOGG. J. No. 4 Coy awarded 14 days F.P. No. 2 ~ 2# for neglect G.C. Bridge.	NP
Mar 20 V.2.	7/2		No. T/235830 Pte HALL S. No. 2 Coy transferred to M.D. 122nd Depot 6 B.I.	NP
	8/2		No. T/4/21207 Cpl. KENDALL S.H No. 3 Coy transferred to No. 1 Coy / 36792 L/Cpl. KIRK J. No. 1 Coy " " 3 "	NP
	9/2		15' grand awarded 12 G.C Bridge.	NP
	10/2		15' 20 min jerking from Ranks Ame Depot. R.	NP
	11/2		Honours Awards. The undermentioned have been awarded the Grand Decoration as stated. T/4/057476 16 S.M. RILEY P.S. Croix de Guerre a L'ordre Divison S/057673 @ Sgt. GORDON S. Croix de Guerre a L'ordre de Regiment the medals were presented to the above named by Divisional Commander Major General Sir S.T.B. LAWFORD? K.C.B. at GRAMMONT BELGIUM on 11/2/18	NP

Army Form C. 2118.

WAR DIARY
or
INTELLIGENCE SUMMARY.
(Erase heading not required.)

Instructions regarding War Diaries and Intelligence Summaries are contained in F. S. Regs., Part II. and the Staff Manual respectively. Title pages will be prepared in manuscript.

Place	Date	Hour	Summary of Events and Information	Remarks and references to Appendices
GRAMMONT	12th	—	T.H.Ok. move to ENGHIEN. No. 75000.25 Lt PRATT W to 3Cy, Lieutenant Col 8th	W.P
V.P.				
	13th		T.H.Ok. move to HAL.	W.P
ENGHIEN				
HAL.	14th		No 7026131 Cpl SANDON F to + Q Lieutenant GCS 12th T.A. Ok. move to BRAIN L'ALLEUD	W.P
BRAIN L' ALLEUD	15th		T Capt H.B. POLLARD - URQUHART struck off the strength in Riding duty at Base Dept, BOULOGNE. No 73403131 Pte CARNOCHAN J to + Q. Lieutenant 13 Gnr.	W.P
	16th		Opportunity taken to visit battlefield of WATERLOO.	W.P
	17th		J.H.Ok. move to MARBAIS	W.P
MARBAIS	18th		J.H.Ok. move to MAZY	W.P
MAZY	19th		J.H.Ok. move to WARET LE CHAUSSEE	W.P

WAR DIARY
or
INTELLIGENCE SUMMARY

Army Form C. 2118.

Place	Date	Hour	Summary of Events and Information	Remarks and references to Appendices
WARET LE CHAUSSEE	20/11		No. T/529/0 1/S.S.M. HULL J.M. proceed from shore depot. No. T/027/0/ W. SCALLY J. amended R.C.S. 17/11. J.H.Q45 move to HUY.	W.P.
HUY	21/11		Normal routine	W.P.
	22/11		Normal routine	W.P.
	23/11		No. T/026944 A. GATTENS T. No. T/30390 " WHITE F.H. No. T/357504 " JOHNSTON ARNOLD. D.A. } proceeded to U.K. Eng. for demobilisation.	W.P.
	24/11		No. T/342660 A. PLOWDEN V.A.B. proceeded to report to Base Camp Lillefonts SPA in 14Bn. to which of belong for that rate	W.P.

Army Form C. 2118.

WAR DIARY
or
INTELLIGENCE SUMMARY.
(Erase heading not required.)

Instructions regarding War Diaries and Intelligence Summaries are contained in F. S. Regs., Part II. and the Staff Manual respectively. Title pages will be prepared in manuscript.

Place	Date	Hour	Summary of Events and Information	Remarks and references to Appendices
HOY	25/11		No. T/017834 Pt JOHNSTON R " T/039204 " THOMAS S S/027140 NAIRN J T/657156 TAYLOR M } Gardeners Reverted to U.K. this day for Embarkation	M.F
	26/11		T/057257 A/Sgt. MILLER J T/023776 A/ CROWE C.W 36172 Pte SUTTON J.E T/250023 Cpl STOREY E T/057611 Pte OXBERRY J } Gardeners Proceeded to U.K. this day for Embarkation	M.F
	27/11		One 14.9 Low No. 141 on charge of No. 3 Cy. died on 24 Inst.	M.F
	28/11		Two H.D. Low No's 104 + 160 on charge No. 1 Cy transferred 26 Inst.	M.F
	29/11		Two H.D. Low No's 82 + 63 on charge No. 1 + 2 Cy transferred 26 Inst.	M.F
	30/11		No. T/26/527 A MAIR R No. 1 Cy admitted 9 P while on leave in the U.K. on 24/11/16. Church off strength from 24/11/16	M.F

WAR DIARY
or
INTELLIGENCE SUMMARY.

Army Form C. 2118.

Place	Date	Hour	Summary of Events and Information	Remarks and references to Appendices
HUY	3/12		On H.Q. Lorry No.17 – Large No. 4 (9) destroyed 29 Inst. On N.Q. Lorry No.149 – Large No. 3 (9) damaged 30 Inst. The undermentioned Gentlemen proceeded to England 1st day for demobilisation rare struck off strength. T/325674 A. MARSDEN. J. No. 1 Cy T/275700 " NICHOLSON. E " 1 " T/035527 " THOMAS. I " 1 " T/076164 " WILSON P.P " 1 " T/394491 OCCLESHAW. S " 3 " 36230 MORLEY. W.H " 4 "	M

M. Poole
Comdg MT Dr Captain

Army Form C. 2118.

WAR DIARY
or
INTELLIGENCE SUMMARY.
(Erase heading not required.)

Instructions regarding War Diaries and Intelligence Summaries are contained in F.S. Regs., Part II. and the Staff Manual respectively. Title pages will be prepared in manuscript.

41 D Train
Q 33

Place	Date	Hour	Summary of Events and Information	Remarks and references to Appendices
HUY	1/1/19		No. T/23737S A/ Bowes T.M.1/Br. remustered to C.S.1. 31/t/ On 1/1/19 Lives to not died 19/14 29/30 to be.	
	2/1		No. T/23380 M.S.M. PARKE F.C. joined from 1st Cavalry Reserve Park appointed a/S.M. (W. of L) from 1/1/19 until post of Supt. transferred to 140/2 Fd Amb. (Auth. Home Recd EF/9043/A/Q of 28/11/18 r RASC Selm M. Q52/1157/6 of 5/12/18	
	3/1/9		a Reinforcement of 1 for from Brig. Supply Pn. 2 L of C Area Recepn. Camp. 14	
	4/1/19		Honors Award :— Lt Colonel T. Dowling RASC. awarded the Order of the British Empire (Military Division.) (Extract from London Gazette & Appointment of 4/1/19). Absorbment in Depôts — Captain H/MORRIS, R.A.S.C. T/20456 Sgt STIRRUP No 3 Cy Into Escort (Extract from Supplement to London Gazette of 30/12))	

(10340) Wt W.3500/P773 750,000 1/16 E 2888 Forms/C2118/16

Army Form C. 2118.

WAR DIARY
or
INTELLIGENCE SUMMARY.
(Erase heading not required.)

Instructions regarding War Diaries and Intelligence Summaries are contained in F. S. Regs., Part II. and the Staff Manual respectively. Title pages will be prepared in manuscript.

Place	Date	Hour	Summary of Events and Information	Remarks and references to Appendices
HUY	5/1/9.		No. T/7/13335 N/Carter W. No. 1 Coy admitted D. 28/12/18 from Divisional Reception Camp. Struck off. No. T/7/0/60263 N/Colpin R. rejoined from W.O. 3 Ercit Pclass W/C 159	NT
	6/1/9.		Substantial December. Lt. Colonel T. Dowling D.B.E. A.C.S. awarded the Substantial Decoration. (Extract from L.G. Supplement of 2½) Capt. H.S. Love No. 5¹. in charge of No. 1 Coy. succeeded.	
	7/1/9.		No. 4 Coy. arrive at ANDENNE for Germany.	
	8/1/9.		Capt. E.H. Wood A.C.S. demobilised returns on leave to U.K. Struck off strength from 20/18.	
	9/1/9.		No. 2 Coy arrive FF at HUY for Germany or 10/9.	

Army Form C. 2118.

WAR DIARY
or
INTELLIGENCE SUMMARY.

(Erase heading not required.)

Instructions regarding War Diaries and Intelligence Summaries are contained in F. S. Regs., Part II. and the Staff Manual respectively. Title pages will be prepared in manuscript.

Place	Date	Hour	Summary of Events and Information	Remarks and references to Appendices
HUY	5/9		No. 17/3335 N°CARTER W the "G" admitted R. 25/12/11 from Divisional Reception Camp. Church Off.	W.D
			No. 71/662263 B. Culpin R. reported from R. on 8 days' probation Cyp.	
	6/9		Divisional Decoder	
			Lt Colonel T Dowling OBE R.A.S. awarded the General Rosette	W.D
			(Extract from L.G. Dispatches of 29)	
			One N.O. Lowe No 51. on charge of hers C.A. remanded	
	7/9		No 11 Cy return to ANDENNE for Entrainment	R
	8/9		Capt Ethelwood Rack Demobilised October on leave to U.S. on Church Off. Ontrofe from 20%.	W.D
	9/9		No 2 Cy return at HUY for Entrainment in 10%.	W.D

Army Form C. 2118.

WAR DIARY
or
INTELLIGENCE SUMMARY.
(Erase heading not required.)

Instructions regarding War Diaries and Intelligence Summaries are contained in F. S. Regs., Part II. and the Staff Manual respectively. Title pages will be prepared in manuscript.

Place	Date	Hour	Summary of Events and Information	Remarks and references to Appendices
HOY	10/7/19		No. 3 Coy. entrain at HOY for Germany. On N.C.O. Leave No. 110 in charge of No. 1 Coy. Head n. 30/7/19	N.P
	11/7/19		Coy. HQrs. entrain at HOY for COLOGNE, Germany.	N.P
COLOGNE Germany	12/7/19		Coy. HQrs. now at COLOGNE. Transferred 14 Barracks Orderly Room at 5 Bayenthal Gürtel. MARIENBURG, COLOGNE.	N.P
			No. 728637 L/East J No. 2 Coy. transferred to 122 Able M.C.C. Wiesbaden.	
	13/7/19		3 Reinforcement join from Boulogne 8 O.R.	N.P
	14/7/19		Returned to Duty etc.	N.P
			Lt Corl T Dowling 9836 T.O.R.A.S.C. (Retained from appointed 16.4.30 %)	

Army Form C. 2118.

WAR DIARY
or
INTELLIGENCE SUMMARY.
(Erase heading not required.)

Instructions regarding War Diaries and Intelligence Summaries are contained in F.S. Regs., Part II. and the Staff Manual respectively. Title pages will be prepared in manuscript.

Place	Date	Hour	Summary of Events and Information	Remarks and references to Appendices
COLOGNE Germany	15/11		3 Drivers awarded 1st Cl. Badge. No. F/2516 W. Godwin A. granted permission to 3 Groups to 2 b/c Coin. No. 1 Coy return at HUT the Germany Reception Camp, interim.	W.O.
	16/11		Proceeded on Pass. L.Colonel J. Dowling. 4/36.19. R.A.S.C. awarded the Belgian Crown de Guerre. (Extract from Orders October 1917 of 15/7.9.) Brevet A.A. Gray. R.A.S.C. No. 1 Coy. has been demobilised returned to Eire UK. - Struck off strength from 29/11.	W.O.
	17/11		General Routine	W.O.
	18/11		Routine Duties. T/5583 S/Sjt M. PERRY A.R. No. 1 Coy. T/9467 App. SCARRATT F. 2 Awarded the Belgian Croix de Guerre. (Aunt. W.O. Letter No. A.G./12/36 H. 8/19).	W.O.

(10340) Wt W3500/P713 750,000 M15 E 2688 Forms/Carts/16
D.D. & L., London, E.C.

Army Form C. 2118.

WAR DIARY
or
INTELLIGENCE SUMMARY.
(Erase heading not required.)

Instructions regarding War Diaries and Intelligence Summaries are contained in F. S. Regs., Part II. and the Staff Manual respectively. Title pages will be prepared in manuscript.

Place	Date	Hour	Summary of Events and Information	Remarks and references to Appendices
COLOGNE Germany	19/9		No 524953 W.O/Cpl. WALKER S.G. granted free re-engagement.	M.P
	20/9		No 088059 N. FALLAIZE W. No & (B) } Transferred to WRIGHT C.W. " " } H.Q. 12th Coy B.O. T/ 424223	M.P
	21/9		No 5/043970 Sgt KEEFE No 3 Coy promoted to No # C.S.I. 22 1/9 T/96621 N ELLIS R. 2 " " " " 20 1/9	M.P
	22/9		No T/22910 S.S.M. HULL J.M. No 16 Coy Transferred to 1st Cavalry Division H.Q (J)	M.P
	23/9		Honours Awards No T/(1)5#3 T.S.S.M. YORK C.H. No 36 No S4/065125 A.Q.M.Sgt TAYLOR W.P. Co 1.9 Co awarded the M.S.M. (Extract from L.G. Appl 4/1879)	M.P

Army Form C. 2118.

WAR DIARY
or
INTELLIGENCE SUMMARY.
(Erase heading not required.)

Instructions regarding War Diaries and Intelligence Summaries are contained in F. S. Regs., Part II. and the Staff Manual respectively. Title pages will be prepared in manuscript.

Place	Date	Hour	Summary of Events and Information	Remarks and references to Appendices
COLOGNE	24/9		To 7/657961 a/ GREEN S. F/36591 " DAVIES R.W. 7/657387 S/ EVANS R.W. A353 " WILKES L.J. } Proceeded this day to U.K. for demobilisation	N/S
Germany	25/9		Normal Routine	N/S
	26/9		Serv 7/80 P/m Rev 1473-1453 mistook No. (7) November 24/9	N/S
	27/9		No 7/240246 W/A. SAILES J.E. No. (7) November 66S ik say	N/S
	28/9		5/6463 N/A. WALKER J. November 66S 25/9	N/S
	29/9		Normal routine	N/S
	30/9		No F/626190 A/ BAKER W. R. (7) November 66S	N/S
	31/9		Capt. H. MORRIS. R.K. proceed to U.K. demobilisation. M Pool Maj. W for W/ D Col.	N/S

WAR DIARY
or
INTELLIGENCE SUMMARY.

(Erase heading not required.)

Army Form C. 2118.

Bnd Train
Vol 34

Place	Date	Hour	Summary of Events and Information	Remarks and references to Appendices
COLOGNE Germany	1/1/19		No. T405809 A/Cpl. SEATON J.T. No. 1 Coy. } Proceeded to U.K. No. T40440 61 Pte DIBBEN C. " 2 " } for demobilisation	MP
	2/1/19		The M/T from No. 128 in charge Lieut. (G) } proceeded 30/1/19 " " " " " " 136 " " " 3 "	MP
	3/1/19		No. T30058 N. BIRD M. Army H.Q. demobilised whilst on leave in U.K. W.e.f. from 17/1/19	MP
	4/1/19		Lieut. HILL Lost. No. 90 G1. in charge No. 1 (G) proceeded 29/1/19	MP
	5/1/19		No. T5774 L/S/Sgt OATEN A.C. No. 2 G proceeded 29/1/19	MP
	6/1/19		Lieut. HB.C. EMBY R.A.S.C. demobilised whilst on leave No. 9 from 10/1/19 T/20338 L/S/Sgt. PULLEN H. No. 2 G proceeded 31/1/19	MP
	7/1/19		9 O.Rank proceeded on 30/1/9 11/2, rest 7/2.	MP

Army Form C. 2118.

WAR DIARY
or
INTELLIGENCE SUMMARY.
(Erase heading not required.)

Instructions regarding War Diaries and Intelligence Summaries are contained in F.S. Regs., Part II. and the Staff Manual respectively. Title pages will be prepared in manuscript.

Place	Date	Hour	Summary of Events and Information	Remarks and references to Appendices
COLOGNE Germany	8/2/19		No. T/26973 A/Sergt. SMITH G. No. 16 duties of supernumerary in 1st Cameron Highs. born in 5th and transferred Popplestoth (Infantry) Bonn Germany. Burnt place	MP
	9/2/19		Appointments: No. 0515570 A/Cpl BARRY J. to the rank of Lce Cpl with pay from 9th inst. No. 175373 In JORDAN Pte attd Supernumerary list from 9th inst. (Cert. Orig from 10 2/19 incl. Orig from 10 2/19 (Auth Rec P5/6/19574/17 A 2 S Th)	NP
			No. 27729 A/Cpl POMFREY W. on appointment 5 2 inst.	
	10/2/19		No. T/26701 A/ Newey H. Pte ① terminated C.C.S. 5 2 on A.D. No. 147 to camp of No. 3 CO returned 12 inst. Date A.D. Received from 139 to a return to Cpl.	NP

Army Form C. 2118.

WAR DIARY
or
INTELLIGENCE SUMMARY.
(Erase heading not required.)

Instructions regarding War Diaries and Intelligence Summaries are contained in F. S. Regs., Part II. and the Staff Manual respectively. Title pages will be prepared in manuscript.

Place	Date	Hour	Summary of Events and Information	Remarks and references to Appendices
COLOGNE Germany	11/7/19		Men being inoculated & T.C.Belfort	N.P
	12/7/19		1 Sgt, 8 Dvrs from here to T.A. [illegible]	N.P
	13/7/19		No 745821 Cpl Hurst R.J. No 2 Coy transfer to Col 11/7/19 No 701343 L/Cpl Gilbart J. - " - 11/7/19	N.P
	14/7/19		75699 L/Cpl McLoughlin M. [illegible] mustered 13/7/19 08930 D. Young J.N. No 2 - " - 14/7/19 No. R.D. to Col in lieu of Col 1 Coy to Col in lieu of 10 [illegible]	N.P
	15/7/19		No. M40 125 Sgt Sanderson J.A. To & Col Wandsworth [illegible] leave. S/O from 15/7/19 Cont. PASS Lecture 7s M39/579 11.0 p.m. No 730344 A. Shorter F. 7o & Col Kensington Lust Res.	N.P

Army Form C. 2118.

WAR DIARY
or
INTELLIGENCE SUMMARY.
(Erase heading not required.)

Instructions regarding War Diaries and Intelligence Summaries are contained in F. S. Regs., Part II. and the Staff Manual respectively. Title pages will be prepared in manuscript.

Place	Date	Hour	Summary of Events and Information	Remarks and references to Appendices
COLOGNE Germany	16/7/19		No. T/085320 A/Spurle J.W. posted in 15 hrs. from 140th H.L. ant.	
	17/7/19		No. T/36577 A/Walker J } Rejoined on 15th inst. T/241101 " Newey T.H. } from 6.C.D.	
	18/7/19		Moved quarters.	
	19/7/19		No. T/144272 A/Dawes A.W. to "B" transferred 82nd Mobile Vet. Sect. No. T/289991 Pte Bryant H. Vice W.O.R. transferred to No. 3 Cy.	
	20/7/19		T/Lieut C.J. Bloodworth, R.A.S.C. joined from 2nd Cavalry Dn. Rems No. T/86149 A/Shepherd A do	
	21/7/19		The undermentioned proceeded to U.K. on 20 days l.f.a. demobilisation. T/37083 Cpl Giss W.H. No. 1 Cy S/4314146 Pte Evans J.H. T/9109 L/Cpl Patrick C.E " T/215127 " Pulkington S.J. S/SR 7/12 L/Cpl James E T.Hok. T/394499 " McCann W.J. T/13/6 L/Cpl Brown W.H. No. 1 Cy H/24236 Pte Manners W.K.	

WAR DIARY
INTELLIGENCE SUMMARY

Army Form C. 2118.

Place	Date	Hour	Summary of Events and Information	Remarks and references to Appendices
COLOGNE Germany	22/9		No 7865965 Pte N SHIPTON xv No 4 Coy awarded 28 days FP No 2 for disobeying the Camp to WK	MR
	23/9		No 6057370 Pte YOUNG J M } rejoin from G.B.S on 20.9.19. No 062215 offr HURST R.J.	MR
	24/9		2nd Lt J CAVANAGH promoted T/Lieut. (Extract from Supp to L.G. of 21/8/19).	MR
	25/9		No Lt 0914250 H KAY W No 1 Coy awarded 28 days FP No 2 for overstaying leave to UK	MR
	26/9		Lieut (T.F.) Major 66 BELL M.C. } join from 46th Div Train 25/9/19. Lieut (T.F.) A. H. ADAMS	MR
	27/9		H Q and transferred to G.G.S.	MR
	28/9		No 73/7605 A/L/Cpl POWELL J. M. G died in No. 21 G.G.S. BONN this day	MR

Commdg 41 Div Train

Army Form C. 2118.

WAR DIARY
or
INTELLIGENCE SUMMARY.
(Erase heading not required.)

Instructions regarding War Diaries and Intelligence Summaries are contained in F. S. Regs., Part II. and the Staff Manual respectively. Title pages will be prepared in manuscript.

Place	Date	Hour	Summary of Events and Information	Remarks and references to Appendices
COLOGNE Germany	1/7/19		2nd Lt. J. BASTON No. 3 Coy. Proceeded U.K. on 29/6. (Extract from Supp. to 2.6.4. of 25/7/19)	M²
	2/7/19		No. 7/3,747 Cpl. SCOTT J.E. demobilised whilst on leave Ho. from 14/6.	M²
			No. T/F/2225 Pte GRANT A.E. No. 1 Coy admitted to R. Infirmary on leave in U.K. Ho. 13/6	
			Two H.A.O. horses No's 4th + 58 in charge No. 1 (?) dismounted 26/6/19	
			One H.A.O. horse No. 4th in charge No. 4 Coy destroyed 28/6/19	
	3/7/19		One H.A.O. No. 150 in charge No. 1 Coy dismounted 30/6/19.	M²
	3/7/19		2nd Lieut R.S. PEACOCK No. 3 Coy to UK on leave 29/6 (Extract from Supp. to 2.6.4. of 28/7/19)	
	5/7/19		One H.A.O. mare in charge No. 3 Coy destroyed.	M²
			One H.A.O. No. 127 mare Ridon No. 7 in charge No. 2 (?) destroyed.	
	6/7/19		S/15/7820 Pte EDKINS F.G. Trans. HAR. No. 1 Coy — Proceeded for demobilisation this day.	M²
			T/30561 THORPE J.	
			T/065330 Dr SPURLE J.W.	
			S/035651 Cpl. WINKLEY A.E. 2.	
			T/337948 Cpl. BREWER C. 3.	

WAR DIARY
or
INTELLIGENCE SUMMARY.
(Erase heading not required.)

Army Form C. 2118.

Place	Date	Hour	Summary of Events and Information	Remarks and references to Appendices
COLOGNE Germany	7/3/19		No: T/261678 Pte BLUNDELL F. T T/233063 Pte JONES J.H. Transferred from 2nd mt transferred to No1 Coy with effect from 6th inst	M?
	8/3/19		One Rider No 3 on charge No 4 Coy destroyed 6th inst. One Rider No 5 in charge No 3 Coy to this day	
	9th		T/124-953 Cpl. Cpl WALKER S.G. No 2 Coy evacuates CCS 9th inst	M?
	10th		T/059889 Dr. ORR V. joined from 138th I.A. Amb.	M.O
	11th		10 Ranks awarded 1st G.C. Badge	M?
	12th		One Rider No 12 & 2 H.T. No's 49 & 118 on charge No1Coy evacuates 11th inst.	M?
	13		1 Col 915 LORY V.S.O. joined from the 25th Divisional Train 1 Cart T. YOWLING OSE. T.V. proceeded to/on 25th Divl Train	M?
	14th		One H.T. No 33 on charge No 4 Coy died 12th inst	M?
	15th		Appointments :- T.S./3655 Gnr. Dr. POWRY J.A. 139th F.A. appointed A/Cpl. from 20/3/19	M?
	16th		Two Riders No's 9 & 147, One H.D. No 51 on charge No1 Coy evacuates 15 inst	M?
	17th		No Instruction Sgt HALLIDAY W.H. No 4 Coy proceed for the Brigadier Hosp.	M?
	18th		One H.D. No 44 on charge of No4 Coy evacuates 15th inst	M?

WAR DIARY
or
INTELLIGENCE SUMMARY
(Erase heading not required.)

Army Form C. 2118.

Instructions regarding War Diaries and Intelligence Summaries are contained in F. S. Regs., Part II. and the Staff Manual respectively. Title pages will be prepared in manuscript.

Place	Date	Hour	Summary of Events and Information	Remarks and references to Appendices
COLOGNE Germany			Appointments	
	19/12		No. TH/041401 Pte BURNISTON E. N/Cpl appt d/Cpl from 26/12/18. TS/19472 Pte Br FURNIVAL H. 138 FA. appt d/Paid Cpl " 18/12/18	W.D.
	20th		Duty:- RQSR P/58/19180 Cpl on leave 9/3/19.	W.D.
			One R.D. No 88 on charge No 1 Coy & sent to the Central Collecting Coy P/58/19180 Cpl Richer " 4 " " " " Coy & Coy ground	W.D.
	21st		Usual routine	W.D.
	22nd		Usual routine	W.D.
	23rd		T4/245859 CQMS JOHNSTON A. No 2 Coy } Demobilized whilst on leave T/356607 Dvr PIKE F " " " in the United Kingdom	W.D.
	24th		One N.O. No. 42 on charge of No 4 Coy evacuated distained	W.D.
	25th		The undermentioned proceeded for demobilization this day T/118515 Sgt VOSPER G.S. } No 4 Coy T/09+205 Pte DAVIS C.H. } 19/SR 0198 " HOWARD H.	W.D.
	26/3/		One R.D. received from H.Q.R. & Co. Bde. 20/3/19	W.D.
	27/3/		No. TF/65.293 L/S ROSIER A. No. 3 Coy transferred to H.Q.R. 123rd Inf Bde	W.D.

Army Form C. 2118.

WAR DIARY
or
INTELLIGENCE SUMMARY.
(Erase heading not required.)

Place	Date	Hour	Summary of Events and Information	Remarks and references to Appendices
COLOGNE Germany	28/3/19		No. T/1242 A/ MARTINDALE F.W. No. 1 Coy tried by F.G.C.M. on 19/3/19 on charge of Drunkeness. Accused was found guilty sentenced to 28 days F.P. No. 2.	MP
	29/3/19		No. T/365.38 Pte WILSON G. No. 1 Coy. evacuated to No. 64 C.C.S. 26/3/19. Two R&D have received from 126th Bde. A.T.A. on 21/3/19	MP
	30/3/19		Usual routine	MP
	31/3/19		Usual routine. Designation of Division changed to London Division 15/3/19.	MP

M Hook Capt. L.L.C.
Comdg London Div. Train.

Army Form C. 2118.

WAR DIARY
or
INTELLIGENCE SUMMARY.
(Erase heading not required.)

Instructions regarding War Diaries and Intelligence Summaries are contained in F. S. Regs., Part II. and the Staff Manual respectively. Title pages will be prepared in manuscript.

Place	Date	Hour	Summary of Events and Information	Remarks and references to Appendices
COLOGNE	1/1/19		Capt E.R.M.MORTON joined from 18 Cdn Tran 2 7/3	BROWN
Germany	2/1/19		Capt W.R.ROBERSON.M.C. " " 19 " " 2 7/3	BROWN
	3/1/19		Lieut G.C.COOKE " " 20 " " 2 7/3	BROWN
			Capt W.R.ROBERSON.M.C. & 2/Lt. E.C.COOKE posted to No 3 Co - 2 7/3. S/M/46290 Sgt. GOODMAN A. to 2 Co remuster Cpl.S. 1 7/3 No 35763 M CHELL J. joined from 18 Cdn Tran 2 7/3	CRM
	4/1/19		Capt/Capt M. POOLES proceeded for instruction in his duty	
			Capt E.R.M. MORTON assumes duty on Adjutant this day	
			Two riders transferred from T.H.Q. to No.1 Co	CRM
	5/1/19		Capt T.V.FLEMING M.C. + a/Capt G.H.COLEGRAVE transferred 6-19°	
			to 2 Co. Tran respectively	
			A/Cpl W.S.MAULE transferred from T/R Apx to command No 4 Co	
			No T/OR 219 a/Cpl Co promoted Cpl. No T/OR656 a/Sgt KENT.T. promoted Sgt	
			No 75/244771 a/Sgt WHEAL C. promoted Sgt. Pvt RASC Jackson P. No 6/20338	BROWN

Army Form C. 2118.

WAR DIARY
or
INTELLIGENCE SUMMARY.
(Erase heading not required.)

Instructions regarding War Diaries and Intelligence Summaries are contained in F.S. Regs., Part II. and the Staff Manual respectively. Title pages will be prepared in manuscript.

Place	Date	Hour	Summary of Events and Information	Remarks and references to Appendices
COLOGNE Germany.	5/7/19		Lt.Col. Capt. J.W.P. NORMAN, joined from 20 Div Train. No. T/3 024012 W. LILLEY J. joined from 20 Div Train. Major W.R. ROBERSON, M.C. assumed command of the 2/G9.	ERNN
	6/7/19		T/3 02962 Cpls MILLS W. M/G seconded to 66 S. s/y T/2 45393 L/cpl WALKER S.G. reported from 66 S.	ERNN
	7/7/19 8/7/19		Usual routine —ditto—	ERNN
	9/7/19		M/J. CAVANAGH Transferred to the HIGHLAND Div TRAIN	ERNN
	10/7/19		T3/044 234 Pte PATRICK R. No 1 Cy. invalided to 66 S. Rein. 1 Dr. awarded 1st Gl Badge.	ERNN
	11/7/19 12/7/19		Capt. G. Tripp No. 2 Cy proceeded for demobilisation this day	ERNN
	13/7/19		1 Driver join from the 38 Div. Train this day	ERNN

Army Form C. 2118.

WAR DIARY
or
INTELLIGENCE SUMMARY.
(Erase heading not required.)

Instructions regarding War Diaries and Intelligence Summaries are contained in F. S. Regs., Part II. and the Staff Manual respectively. Title pages will be prepared in manuscript.

Place	Date	Hour	Summary of Events and Information	Remarks and references to Appendices
COLOGNE Germany	14/9/19		On HQ no 119 a Larger No. 1 G delivered	AA/S
	15/9/19		11 Joining from the General Ou Train	
			No. F/556631 A/Cpl. Pr. No. 1 G recounted GSW 14⅔	
			" 085397 " Young Wm " 2 " -do- 2⅖	CUSS
			Capt. Adj. E.R.M. MORTON transferred to Light Ou Train	
			Captain W.A. WEBBER-BROWN joined from Light Ou Train & assumed duty as Adjutant	
	16/9/19		on 16 inst	
			No T/37042 S. POWER E joined — 13 Ind from Light Ou Train	AA/S
			" H 26463 " CHELL J transferred to Light Ou Train 15 Inst	
			" T 22536 Cpl CHIDGAY H. Sn 2 G. discharged with no line a US	
			Sn from 8⅔ Austr Regt 423/13619 49 ⅔	
	17/9/19		22 Grands from General Ou Train	AA/S
			S/018023 L/Sgt LEACH Jn. 1 921893 Cpl SMITH J join from 20 Co Ou Train.	
	18/9/19		731 BC RUSSELL Robt. joined for 17 Co Ou Train	
			Major D.G. PARKER Robt. proceed on leave for Great Britain for 1 month	AA/S
			Sp from 27 3/4.	

(A9979) Wt. W2355/1560 500,000 12/17 D. D. & L. Sch. 82— Forms/C2118/15.

Army Form C. 2118.

WAR DIARY
or
INTELLIGENCE SUMMARY.
(Erase heading not required.)

Instructions regarding War Diaries and Intelligence Summaries are contained in F. S. Regs., Part II. and the Staff Manual respectively. Title pages will be prepared in manuscript.

Place	Date	Hour	Summary of Events and Information	Remarks and references to Appendices
COLOGNE Germany	19/7/19		13/22359 A/Sergt ? ho-m(?) transfered to H.Q.R. 31st Infan. Bde.	A/S
			M/068054 A/Holden W transferred to H.Q.R. 3rd Inf. Bde.	
			H/308493 A/Turnbull A Escort du Troops Arrival from 6th CCS	
			H/36476 D/Bell H E. proceed from 20 CCS on leave	
			H/38460 N Conroy WT Pvt 3 Cy transferred to 3/ "C.C.S	
	20/7/19		M/ C.S. Stephen proceed from Canaan Christian 14 Coast	A/S
			One N.O. Cpl 329 class "B" to charge of No 2 Cy	
	21/7/19		T/186262 Cpl ELLARD H.J. No. 2 Cy Depot HQ-AMS 12/7/19 medically unfit for	A/S
			the Mississippi to MMS. Johnson on discharge	
			Capt. Rusf Q.63/2114 of 15/7/19.	A/S
	22/7/19		No T/324621 D/ Vincent Frank (?) Cy. transferred to 20 CCS in lieu... (?)	W/S
	23/7/19		Usual Routine	
	24/7/19		Major R. Locke D.S.O. joined from H.Q. Owl Train 22nd inst & posted to 1 Coy.	W/S
			S/213856 Booth Alfred joined from 38th Div Train 23rd inst.	
			T/389121 Pte McPowell joined from 20th Div Train 23rd inst.	
			T/364662 Pte Newell joined from 20th Div Train 24th inst.	

Army Form C. 2118.

WAR DIARY
or
INTELLIGENCE SUMMARY.
(Erase heading not required.)

Instructions regarding War Diaries and Intelligence Summaries are contained in F. S. Regs., Part II. and the Staff Manual respectively. Title pages will be prepared in manuscript.

Place	Date	Hour	Summary of Events and Information	Remarks and references to Appendices
COLOGNE Germany.	25/1/19		Inspection by O.C. London Division Transport & Billets	Wks
	26/1/19		T/4/215417 Pte Smith H joined from 20th Bus train 26th inst	
	27/1/19		Usual Routine	
	28/1/19		T/387121 Pte Powell H, T/308193 Pte Tucker H, T/307 Cpl Gryfoot H.O., T/326 Pte Angola N. T/45328 Pte Brand W.A. T/307060 Pte Campbell G, T/408301 Pte Redshaw J.E. T/065301 Cpl Green J, ET/454500 Pte Randoroough R.R. T/8125 Pte West R. ET/484167 Pte Corp. Kirk J. ET/48183 Pte Heritage W.H. having ceased for demobilization are struck off the strength 26th inst.	C.Wks
			and M.O. Nr 60 Slave L.R. Evacuated & Struck off 22nd inst.	
	29/1/19		1/Major R.E.F. Launder. D.S.O.R.A.S.C. joined from western Divisional train 28th inst.	Wks
	30/1/19		T/3265 Pte Wicker R. joined from western Divl. Troop 28th inst 3 M.10 Horses joined from London Divl. Animal Reception Camp 29th inst	Wks

W. de Bush Capt for
COMMANDING
LONDON DIVISIONAL TRAIN, R.A.S.C.

Army Form C. 2118.

WAR DIARY
or
INTELLIGENCE SUMMARY.
(Erase heading not required.)

Place	Date	Hour	Summary of Events and Information	Remarks and references to Appendices
MARIENBURG CÖLN GERMANY.	1st May.		General Routine	
	2nd		General Routine Major P.W Rocklin DSO to 35th But Train Lieut W. Adam to 17th But Train Major R&G Saunders DSO assumed the duties of SSO London to in place of Major P.W Rocklin DSO	
	3rd		General Routine	
	4th		General Routine	
	5th		General Routine	
	6th		General Routine	
	7th		General Routine	
	8th		General Routine	
	9th		General Routine	
	10th		General Routine Lieut Lo Cock R.A.F. passed from Midlan to in personal rain 9th inst	
	11th		General Routine	
	12th		General Routine	

Army Form C. 2118.

WAR DIARY
INTELLIGENCE SUMMARY.
(Erase heading not required.)

Instructions regarding War Diaries and Intelligence Summaries are contained in F. S. Regs., Part II. and the Staff Manual respectively. Title pages will be prepared in manuscript.

Place	Date	Hour	Summary of Events and Information	Remarks and references to Appendices
MARIENBORG, CÖLN GERMANY	10th		General Routine	WDSW
	11th		General Routine	WDSW
	15th		Lieut. & Qr. M.C. Rast att. 8/13 East Surrey Regt. joined for duty 13th inst.	WDSW
	16th		General Routine	WDSW
	17th		General Routine	WDSW
	18th		General Routine	WDSW
	19th		General Routine	WDSW
	20th		General Routine	WDSW
	21st		1/2 W.1169 15.10 Satchell transferred to h.91. Leav London but Train 21st inst	WDSW
	22nd		General Routine	WDSW
	23rd		Capt 9 Agr. Lt. Col. Wilkey Mason proceeded for Demobilization 23rd inst	WDSW
	24th		Capt. W.D. Horman to be Adjutant vice Lt/Col Capt. O.a.P.O. Weber Brown	WDSW
	25th		General Routine	WDSW
	26th		T/d/2883 15. J. A. Sansom. T/260636 15 Mutton W.T. proceeded for Demobilization 23rd inst	WDSW
	27th		General Routine	WDSW

Army Form C. 2118.

WAR DIARY
or
INTELLIGENCE SUMMARY.
(Erase heading not required.)

Instructions regarding War Diaries and Intelligence Summaries are contained in F. S. Regs., Part II. and the Staff Manual respectively. Title pages will be prepared in manuscript.

Place	Date	Hour	Summary of Events and Information	Remarks and references to Appendices
MARIENBURG	28t		General Routine	
CÖLN GERMANY	29t		Lieut R.S. Peacock R.A.S.C. proceeded for demobilization 27th inst. Lieut W. Pickford R.A.S.C to Supply Officer 1st London Infantry Bde Lieut A.S. Shepherd R.A.S.C to Supply Officer 2nd London Infantry Bde	
	30t		General Routine	
	31st		General Routine.	

1st June 1919

T.W.D. Newman
CAPT. & ADJUTANT
LONDON DIVISIONAL TRAIN R.A.S.C.

Army Form C. 2118.

WAR DIARY
INTELLIGENCE SUMMARY.
(Erase heading not required.)

Instructions regarding War Diaries and Intelligence Summaries are contained in F. S. Regs., Part II. and the Staff Manual respectively. Title pages will be prepared in manuscript.

Place	Date	Hour	Summary of Events and Information	Remarks and references to Appendices
MARIENBERG COLN. GERMANY.	1/1/19		General Routine.	nil.
	2/1/19		General Routine. T/4/037931 Pte. BRADLEY F.C. No.1 Coy. Admitted to Hospital whilst on leave to U.K. and struck off Strength.	
			T/3/024084. Coy/L. JOHNSON W.J. appointed C.Q.M.S.	
			T/4/5181234. Coy/L. HATCH G.B. " Sergt.	
			T/4/041954. " DENNY B.M. " Sergt.	
			T/4/041011. L/Coy/L BURNISTON E " Coy/L.	
			T/4/026626. " KNOWLTON C " Coy/L.	
			T/125142. " COCKBURN T " Coy/L.	
			T/410993. " CHETLAND A " L/Coy/L.	
			T/324949 " LUNTLEY C.W " L/Coy/L.	
			T/4/060903 " SWANN W " L/Coy/L.	
	3/1/19		General Routine. T/Lieut. B.C. RUSSELL R.A.S.C. posted to No. 3 Company.	nil.
			T/Lieut. R.W. MAYSON R.A.S.C. " " 4 "	
			T/Lieut. G.W. BAGOT. R.A.S.C. Joined from A.H.T.D. ABBEVILLE. 2.6.19.	
			One Indian transferred from Main Bdegs to No. 1 Company.	
			T/409972. Pte. CASEY M.P. transferred from No. 1 Coy. to No. 4 Coy.	
			T/4/099932. C.Q.M.S. MILLS W. returned to duty from Gend Reinforcement Base dépôt.	nil.
	4/1/19		General Routine. T/336424. Pte. STANNARD E.G. Joined from 14th Army Auxce (Co) Coy.	nil.

Army Form C. 2118.

WAR DIARY
INTELLIGENCE SUMMARY.
(Erase heading not required.)

Instructions regarding War Diaries and Intelligence Summaries are contained in F.S. Regs. Part II. and the Staff Manual respectively. Title pages will be prepared in manuscript.

Place	Date	Hour	Summary of Events and Information	Remarks and references to Appendices
MARIENBERG COLN GERMANY.	5/9/19.		General Routine. 7/33404 Cpl. DARKE W.F. joined from 15th Army Awd. (to Coy) from hq. 2 Coy. T/P/083062 a/Cpl. DRYSDALE T transferred from hq. 4 Coy. to hq. 2 Coy.	gmsw.
	6/9/19.		General Routine.	gmsw.
	7/9/19.		General Routine. T/105.85.495 Cpl. BOLTON J.J. applied Sergt. T/5/153.43 L/Cpl. JORDAN J.W. applied Cpl. T/3/24015 Dr. PARKER W " Cpl. T/4/110334 Dr. BURLING J " Cpl. T/35R284/8 " OXLEY J " L/Cpl " WILSON F " L/Cpl. T/3/890 Sam. R. Sgt. WATSON A " Sam. R. Sgt. T/4/95196 " L/Cpl. PARSONS D " L/Cpl. B. Sgt. T/5/964 W/S Lt. PRATT A.E. " W/S Cpl. T/6/1035 Sam. R. MARSHALL J " Sam. Cpl. T/4/143066 Sadd.Cpl NOBLE H.W. " Sadd.Cpl. S/404302 S/S COLLARD H.G. " Cpl. Conf. to D. Horse No. 441, Class BY, evacuated to No. 52nd hy. V.6 and struck off strength.	gmsw.
	8/9/19.		General Routine. Conf. to D. Horse No. 231, Class AX, died and struck off strength.	gmsw.
	9/9/19.		General Routine. T/5/1590 Sam R Sgt. WATSON A. to 1. Coy. transferred to No. 2. Coy. Sadd B. Cpl. STURGESS A.G. awarded M.S.M. Y/19266.	gmsw.
	10/9/19.		General Routine. T/4/094234 Dr. SELWICK B. joined from General Reinforcement Base Depot. and posted to No. 1. Coy. Two H.D. Horses drawn from Advd. Remount Section one L.D. 52nd hy. Vety. Section.	gmsw.
	11/9/19.		General Routine.	gmsw.

Army Form C. 2118.

WAR DIARY
INTELLIGENCE SUMMARY.
(Erase heading not required.)

Instructions regarding War Diaries and Intelligence Summaries are contained in F.S. Regs., Part II. and the Staff Manual respectively. Title pages will be prepared in manuscript.

Place	Date	Hour	Summary of Events and Information	Remarks and references to Appendices
MARIENBURG. COLN. GERMANY.	12/6/19		General Routine.	msr
	13/6/19		General Routine. T4/280440 D/r Juniper W. J. transferred to Codgrs. 2nd London Inf. Bde. T4/262454. "PEACE R."	msr.
	14/6/19		General Routine.	msr.
	15/6/19		General Routine.	msr.
	16/6/19		General Routine. T4/242362. D/r Haines A.E. 2nd Cavalry Reserve Park joined from Rhine Army Reception Camp. One to D. Coase No.141 Class C/t. evacuated to 52nd A.V.D.	msr.
	17/6/19		General Routine. T/Lieut. C.H. Battle R.A.S.C. joined from G.H.Q.	msr.
	18/6/19		General Routine. T4/262101 D/r Schofield L joined from 14th Army Auxol (Co) Co. St DH4584. Lt Bosomworth E. No.1 Coy. transferred to No.4 Coy. No.3 Coy. move to Engelskirchen area will Brigade Group 1	msr.
	19/6/19		General Routine. Nos 2 and 4 Coys move to Overath Area will respective Bde. Groups.	msr.

Army Form C. 2118.

WAR DIARY

INTELLIGENCE SUMMARY.

(Erase heading not required.)

Place	Date	Hour	Summary of Events and Information	Remarks and references to Appendices
MARIENBERG	20/6		General Routine	msv
CÖLN	21/6		General Routine	msv
GERMANY	22/6		General Routine	msv
	23/6		General Routine	msv
	24/6		General Routine	msv
	25/6		General Routine	msv
	26/6		General Routine	msv
	27/6		General Routine. Lieut N.9 LEWIS joined 27th posted to N.º 2 troop.	msv
	28/6		General Routine. Lieut B.M. BAILLIE proceeded for demobilization 27th inst.	msv
	29/6		General Routine	msv
	30/6		General Routine Nº 2 & 3 Coys. Returned to HEUMAR.	msv

Instructions regarding War Diaries and Intelligence Summaries are contained in F. S. Regs., Part II. and the Staff Manual respectively. Title pages will be prepared in manuscript.

Army Form C. 2118.

WAR DIARY
or
INTELLIGENCE SUMMARY.
(Erase heading not required.)

Instructions regarding War Diaries and Intelligence Summaries are contained in F. S. Regs. Part II. and the Staff Manual respectively. Title pages will be prepared in manuscript.

Place	Date	Hour	Summary of Events and Information	Remarks and references to Appendices
MARIENBURG COLN GERMANY	1/7/19		General Routine	mov
	2/7/19		General Routine	mov
	3/7/19		Lieut C J Aberdwooth Admitted Hospital 2nd mct. General Routine	mov
	4/7/19		General Routine	mov
	5/7/19		General Routine	mov
	6/7/19		General Routine	mov
	7/7/19		General Routine	mov
	8/7/19		General Routine	mov
	9/7/19		General Routine	mov
	10/7/19		General Routine	mov
	11/7/19		General Routine	mov
	12/7/19		General Routine Lieut L J Aberdwooth Discharged Hospital 11th mct.	mov
	13/7/19		General Routine	mov
	14/7/19		General Routine	mov
	15/7/19		General Routine	mov
	16/7/19		Lieut G C Scott Discharged Hospital 14th and transferred to Midland Bar Train 14th	mov

WAR DIARY
or
INTELLIGENCE SUMMARY.
(Erase heading not required.)

Army Form C. 2118.

Instructions regarding War Diaries and Intelligence Summaries are contained in F. S. Regs., Part II. and the Staff Manual respectively. Title pages will be prepared in manuscript.

Place	Date	Hour	Summary of Events and Information	Remarks and references to Appendices
MARIENBURG CO-LN	14/7/19		General Routine	
GERMANY	15/7/19		General Routine	
	16/7/19		General Routine	
	17/7/19		General Routine	
	21/7/19		General Routine	
	22/7/19		General Routine	
	23/7/19		General Routine	
	24/7/19		General Routine	
	25/7/19		General Routine	
	26/7/19		General Routine	
	27/7/19		General Routine	
			General Routine. 2/Lieut J.S. Steward to command No. 1 Coy. / Captain W. S. Houle to No. 4	
	28/7/19		Posted to No. 1 Coy	
	29/7/19		General Routine	
	30/7/19		General Routine	
	31/7/19		General Routine 2/Lieut H.G. Lewis proceeded for demobilization 30th Movement London but from 11/8/19	

Army Form C. 2118.

WAR DIARY
or
INTELLIGENCE SUMMARY.
(Erase heading not required.)

Instructions regarding War Diaries and Intelligence Summaries are contained in F. S. Regs., Part II. and the Staff Manual respectively. Title pages will be prepared in manuscript.

Place	Date	Hour	Summary of Events and Information	Remarks and references to Appendices
COLN GERMANY	1/3/19		General Routine	9 nov
	2/3/19		General Routine	2 nov
	3/3/19		General Routine	9 nov
	4/3/19		General Routine	9 nov
	5/3/19		General Routine	9 nov
	6/3/19		General Routine	9 nov
	7/3/19		General Routine	9 nov
	4/3/19		General Routine	9 nov
	5/3/19		General Routine	9 nov
	8/3/19		General Routine	9 nov
	9/3/19		General Routine	9 nov
	10/3/19		General Routine	9 nov
	11/3/19		General Routine	9 nov
	12/3/19		General Routine 1/Cpl W S Paterson proceeded for demobilization	9 nov
			11 mol	
	13/3/19		General Routine	9 nov
	14/3/19		General Routine	m nov
	15/3/19		General Routine	9 nov

Army Form C. 2118.

WAR DIARY
of
INTELLIGENCE SUMMARY.
(Erase heading not required.)

Instructions regarding War Diaries and Intelligence Summaries are contained in F. S. Regs., Part II. and the Staff Manual respectively. Title pages will be prepared in manuscript.

Place	Date	Hour	Summary of Events and Information	Remarks and references to Appendices
	1/9/19		General Routine	
	2/9/19		General Routine	
	3/9/19		General Routine	
	14/9/19		General Routine	
			General Routine	
	21/9/19		General Routine	
	22/9/19		General Routine	
	23/9/19		General Routine	
	24/9/19		General Routine	
	25/9/19		General Routine	
	26/9/19		General Routine	
	27/9/19		General Routine	
	28/9/19		General Routine	
	29/9/19		General Routine	
	30/9/19		General Routine	
			General Routine	

Army Form C. 2118.

WAR DIARY
or
INTELLIGENCE SUMMARY.
(Erase heading not required.)

Instructions regarding War Diaries and Intelligence Summaries are contained in F. S. Regs., Part II. and the Staff Manual respectively. Title pages will be prepared in manuscript.

Place	Date	Hour	Summary of Events and Information	Remarks and references to Appendices
Mauersburg Cologne	1919 Sept 1		General Routine	
"	" 2		General Routine	
"	" 3		General Routine	
"	" 4		General Routine	
"	" 5		Lieut P.W. Mayson transferred from No. 4 Coy R.A.S.C. to Light Drawsonal Train	
"	" 6		General Routine	
"	" 7		Lieut F.E. Aaronson transferred from Light Draf Train to No. 4 Company R.A.S.C	
"	" 7		General Routine	
"	" 8		Capt. W.J. Wade from No. 1 Coy to No. 2 Coy as Supply Officer	
"	" 9		General Routine	
"	" 9		Lieut W.A. Scott body from No. 2 Coy to 22nd M.T. Reception Park on the 9th.	
"	" 10		General Routine	
"	" 10		S/4.070.722 Sergt W. Smithurst proceeded for Demobilization on the 10th	
"	" 11		General Routine	
"	" 11		T/32.656 Dr. P. Worby proceeded for Demobilization on the 5th.	
"	" 12		General Routine	
"	" 13		General Routine	
"	" 14		General Routine	
"	" 15		General Routine	
"	" 16		General Routine	
			Carried Forward	

Army Form C. 2118.

WAR DIARY
or
INTELLIGENCE SUMMARY.
(Erase heading not required.)

Place	Date	Hour	Summary of Events and Information	Remarks and references to Appendices
Marienburgh Cologne	1919 Sept 17		General Routine	mm
"	" 18		General Routine	mm
"	" 19		General Routine	mm
"	" 20		General Routine	mm
"	" 21		General Routine	mm
"	" 22		Capt J Logan Bell taken on strength and posted to No 4 Coy R.A.S.C	mm
"	" 23		Lieut-Col F.B. Lord D.S.O admitted Hospital on the 22nd	mm
"	" 24		General Routine	mm
"	" 25		Lieut J.L Cranfield R.A.S. transferred from H¼ at M.T.E. London Sup. Train Head quarters. Bt Major A.L Madroy to G.H.Q for temporary duty. Lt Abrams to No 1 Coy for temporary duty	mm
"	" 26		Capt J.E Thoecher from 1st Cavalry Sup Col R.A.S.C to No 1 Coy R.A.S.C Lon. Sup. Train	mm
"	" 27		Lieut A/Capt relinquished the rank of A/Capt on being transferred from H¼ M.T.E to Div. Train	mm
"	" 28		General Routine	mm
"	" 29		General Routine	mm
"	" 30		General Routine	mm
			Lieut-Col F.B. Lord D.S.O discharged from Hospital on the 30th	mm

Mo45 Wt. W11422/M160 35,000 12/16 D. D. & L. Forms/C/2118/14.

Army Form C. 2118.

WAR DIARY
or
INTELLIGENCE SUMMARY.

Headquarters London Divisional Train R.A.S.C.

(Erase heading not required.)

Instructions regarding War Diaries and Intelligence Summaries are contained in F. S. Regs., Part II. and the Staff Manual respectively. Title pages will be prepared in manuscript.

Place	Date	Hour	Summary of Events and Information	Remarks and references to Appendices
MERZENBURG COLOGNE	1-12.13-10-19		Routine as Usual.	
	14-10-19		K/101595 Pte J Howard & 511967 Pte Pte W.B. proceeded to the U.K. for demobilisation	
	15-10-19		T/Cpl Gardiner G.H. " " " "	
	16-10- 27-10-19		Routine as Usual	
	27-10-19		T/10.54/216566 C/S M Wise proceeded to the U.K.	
			T.2.S/44 7297 A/Sergt Scott T. S S/45746 Pte Caswell E.M. proceeded to the U.K. for demobilisation.	
	29-10-19		1/Lieut F.L. Cranfield transferred to A.S.B. Cologne for duty.	
	28.10. 31-10-19		Routine as usual	

[signature]
CAPT. & ADJUTANT
LONDON DIVISIONAL TRAIN R.1

41st. DIVISIONAL TRAIN, A.S.C.

Statement of Casualties, from May 1916 to 30th. Septr. 1917.

Killed.

2/Lt. G. Warrington, A.S.C.   Killed 13/3/17.

T2/11241. Corpl. Hastings D.   "   23/5/17.

T4/094275. Driver Milburn J.   Died of wounds. 23/5/17.

T4/233314.   "   Wiggins G.W. Killed. 4/3/17.

Wounded.

Lieut. W.S. Maile. A.S.C.   Wounded 30/4/17.

2/Lieut. S. Cookson A.S.C.   "   13/3/17.

T4/062033. Driver Cox J.   "   6/1/17.

T3/026537.   "   Stevens J.C. "   6/1/17.

T/36543.   "   Minshull J. "   23/5/17.

T1/4373.   "   Cullen P.   "   27/7/17.

T3/027002. Sgt. Hamilton A.   "   7/3/17.

Gassed.

T2/SR/03774. Driver Steel C.J.   Gassed. 1/6/17.

T/23223.   "   Grant W.E.   "   1/6/17.

T4/057437.   "   Churchill W.A.M. "   4/6/17.

Horses. Killed.

9.

Horses. Wounded.

21.

Casualties to Vehicles.

Totally destroyed.   5.

Evacuated.   2.

Repaired in Field.   7.

W.S. Maile
Captain. for,
Commdg. 41st. Divl: Train.

30th. September 1917.

HISTORICAL RECORD

OF

41st Divisional Train.

296: 297: 298: 299 (H.T.) Coys.

ARMY SERVICE CORPS.

1/France/7.

Appendices
- "A" Commanding Officers
- "B" Honours & Awards.
- "C" Casualties amongst Personnel.
- "D" Casualties amongst Wagons & Horses.
- "E" Company Moves.
- "F" Prizes won by Train.

Formed 15th March 1915.

HISTORICAL RECORD

OF

No. 41 DIVISIONAL TRAIN

296, 297, 298, & 299 C O Ys. (H.T). A. S. C.

APPENDICES.

"A" — COMMANDING OFFICERS.
"B" — HONOURS & AWARDS.
"C" — CASUALTIES AMONGST PERSONNEL.
"D" — CASUALTIES AMONGST WAGONS & HORSES.
"E" — COMPANY MOVES.
"F" — PRIZES WON BY TRAIN.

Recorded by R. Victor Beveridge,
    2/ Lieutenant, A.S.C.
        April 1918.

JB.

HISTORICAL RECORD

OF

No. 41 DIVISIONAL TRAIN

1915.

The Train was formed at ALDERSHOT on March 15th 1915, and moved to FRENSHAM PLACE, near FARNHAM to undergo necessary training and drill; the personnel being composed of newly enlisted men who had passed horsemanship tests at the Depots from which they had been drawn.

It was not for some time after moving to FRENSHAM that horses were first issued to the Train; the first arrived in July and by August nearly 100 Riders and Heavy Draught Horses were in the possession of the Companies. It was found necessary to give further tuition to a number of the men in riding, driving and care in stables.

On September 12th 1915 a move was made to WITLEY CAMP, near GODALMING where mobilization began, and the men were supplied with their full equipment. Rations were drawn for, and delivered to various Units of the Division which were then in course of formation

In November the Train proceeded to WITCHETT NORTH CAMP, ALDERSHOT. but owing to the unfinished state of the

1915.

Camp and the muddy condition of the ground, only six days were spent there. One half of the train moved to PANGBOURNE, while the other half returned to its old quarters at FRENSHAM. The training at this time was very severe, with night marches, and under conditions which might be expected in work at the front.

1916.

Early in February 1916, the whole Train concentrated at WYTCHETT, where supplies were drawn for the whole Division from ALDERSHOT Supply Depot.

On April 26th the Senior Supply Officer with the Train supply officers crossed to France to make advance arrangements for supplying the Division. The No. 1 Train Company embarked at SOUTHAMPTON for HAVRE on May 1st, the other three Companies embarking on the three following days. On arrival at HAVRE, the various companies entrained for STRAZEELE in which area the Division was concentrating.

At the end of May a move was made to LA CRECHE, where railhead was at STEENWERCKE, from which the train drew supplies direct.

Three nights a week here, 30 G.S. wagons were sent up to the trenches with Gas Cylinders. 10 of the Train Wagons were also detached for duty with the Royal Engineers in ARMENTIERES. On July 30th while engaged on this work, one of these wagons, with its pair of horses, was destroyed by enemy shellfire.

1916.

On August 23rd 1916, a move towards the SOMME was started, the Companies moving by train and joining up at LONG. On the railway journey one driver was kicked out of the truck by a mule, and had a leg cut off by the train which was moving at the time. At this place the average day's journey covered twenty-five kilometres.

Early in September the train moved to BUIRE on the SOMME, where the greatest difficulty was experienced in delivering the Artillery rations, wagons with these supplies frequently being out for 24 hours at a stretch. This delay was caused through the terrible congestion of traffic on the roads, to relieve which Train Companies were all sent over mud tracks, across country; it was difficult to locate the artillery horse lines in the darkness of the night and at the same time keep to the ill defined tracks.

Many a time extra horses had to be borrowed from nearby camps or units to help in extricating wagons bogged in bad places, on one occasion a team of twelve horses had to be gathered together to salve one such vehicle.

On September 11th the whole Train moved to the outskirts of ALBERT with railhead at FRICOURT, from which the rations were drawn by horse transport. Owing to the unpunctuality of the pack train, the train wagons often had to wait long periods by the railhead, where a 9.2 Howitzer

1916.

Battery was in position. On one occasion a Train horse dropped dead of shock caused by the Howitzer fire.

For one day railhead was at MONTAUBAN, and in order to get the wagons into the yard a road had to be made by filling up shell holes at the entrance.

On the 16th September, Headquarters and 3 Companies marched by road to HALLENCOURT, staying one night at BUIRE. No. 1 Company of the Train remained to supply the Artillery which was kept in the line. The three Companies entrained at LONGPRE and PONT REMY for CAESTRE, from there marching to quarters in the vicinity of RENINGHELST.

Three weeks later No. 1 Company rejoined the Train having marched the whole journey by road. The trek was a very trying one to the horses after their heavy work on the SOMME, a number of the Artillery horses died on the march through sheer exhaustion.

During the whole time spent at RENINGHELST, supplies were drawn from WIPPENHOEK railhead by the Train Companies.

In December a large quantity of bricks were brought by night from YPRES in order to make standings for the horses.

1917.

At the beginning of 1917 the YPRES Sector had few and bad roads as a rule, one railway line and the beginnings of a trench tramway in the forward area. Camps were often

1917.

quagmires and a considerable portion of the Division was living in Tents. These conditions however, in preparation for the MESSINES operations, steadily improved, as road metal, railway material and timber came forward, and horse standings and wagon lines made of bricks, from the ruins of YPRES and VLAMERTINGHE.

About the middle of April the X Corps Roads Officer required a detachment of 1 Officer, 1 N.C.O. 10 drivers and 20 H.D. horses for road work in the forward area at night. This party suffered heavy casualties, 1 N.C.O. was killed, one man died of wounds, 2 drivers were wounded and 3 gassed, two horses were killed and 1 G.S. wagon blown up. Owing to heavy shelling it was frequently necessary to abandon wagons with their loads and recover them later, often with very great difficulty.

The demand for transport grew so heavy towards the end of May that assistance had to be got from the First Line transport to cope with the work.

Owing to the pipe line being cut on June 7th by shell fire, it was necessary to send up convoys of water carts for two days and nights; these were taken up every six hours full, the empties being brought back for refilling.

The arrangements for taking forward the extra rations provided by Second Army were:- A general dump was made at a position in advance of the railhead prior to the

1917.

6th of June, when the advance was to take place, these were taken forward by the Train and delivered to Brigade Headquarters then in the Line. Captain W.S. Maile was wounded whilst inspecting reserve rations at strong points.

The ordinary supply arrangements were, drawing direct from railhead, dumping, then loading and conveying the rations in the Supply Wagons as far as Unit's wagon lines, thence by 1st Line transport. Occasionally resort had to be made to Pack Transport for conveyance of food, ammunition, etc.

When the Division was withdrawn from the MESSINES operations, and was in rest in the ST. OMER area, one of its battalions was heavily bombed by enemy aircraft when it sustained 100 casualties. No. 4 Company of the Train was in the same Camp and 2/Lieut. G. Warrington was killed, 2/Lieut. S. Cookson being wounded at the same time.

During this period of rest from 22nd August to 16th September 1917, the Divisional Supply Column drew supplies from ST. OMER, the train being at WIZERNES. A return was then made to RENINGHELST with railhead at OUDERDOM where the Train drew direct and often under heavy shell fire. The weather was so appalling that wagons were frequently sent up to the line to bring down infantrymen who were in a state of collapse and almost drowned by the unceasing downpour.

1917.

On the night of September 21st, two of the Train drivers Mellersh and Taylor, were engaged on R.E. Convoy near Jackson's dump, VERBRANDEN ROAD, by ST. ELOI, when it came under heavy shellfire. The unloading party took cover, but Mellersh drew his wagon across the road to prevent Taylor's team from bolting, the two men then unloaded their wagons. For this conduct and devotion to duty the two men were awarded Military Medals.

On September 24th another move was made to CAESTRE, from which, four days later, the Train marched by road to LA PANNE in the coastal area, with railhead at OOST HOUK, from there, on October 7th, a change was made to ST. IDESBALDE, where the supplies were dumped from DECAUVILLE railway.

Owing to the sandy soil of the dunes, where the wagon lines were situated, and to the ever drifting clouds of sand, a good deal of sickness was caused to the horses through sand colic; heavy shelling was also experienced, but fortunately no casaulties were caused thereby.

At the end of October the situation on the Italian Front was such as to necessitate the transfer of British Divisions to that sphere of operations, and the Train moved back to ROSENDALE to prepare and equip for the Italian Campaign.

By the 11th of November all preparations were

1917.

complete, and No. 3 Company entrained at ESQUELBECQ, from which station No. 4 Company also departed. Headquarters and No. 2 Company moved from LOON PLAGE on the 12th, and on that day No. 1 Company entrained at ST. OMER, having marched there by road with the Divisional Artillery.

The average time taken for the train journey to Italy was five days. No. 1 Company, with the Artillery detrained at the Italian frontier, and completed their march by road to SAVONA, entraining there to join the Division, arriving several days after the Infantry Units.

One day's rations was carried on supply wagons which travelled on each train, on detraining the Units took these wagons with the extra days' rations, and the Train then collected these vehicles and took up the ordinary routine of supply work.

As the Supply Column marched by road and did not arrive for some days after the Division moved up to the line, which it did before concentration was complete, Italian motor lorries had to be obtained to draw from railhead. For three days the pack train did not arrive and supplies had to be secured from the Italian authorities.

On November 19th the Train started the journey up Country from ACQUANEGRA. As a number of machine guns and trench mortars had to be carried, four civilian wagons,

1917.

horses and drivers, were hired for each Brigade and these were kept with the Train for three or four weeks on the Trek.

The final destination, SELVA, at the foot of the MONTELLO was reached on December 3rd. Until the units were all joined to the Division, there was much difficulty in ascertaining where these arrived and where they were, as detraining points were different as the Division advanced. This difficulty was however surmounted and no unit had to go without its rations, though it was frequently late before the locations were found. The supply column got up with the Division three days after it set out for the Front.

On the MONTELLO, on the other side of which the first line lay, there were a number of small farms which had been abandoned by their owners; on these quantities of hay had been left and at night the Train wagons went out to collect as much of this forage as possible. This was a very trying duty owing to the bad and hilly roads aggravated by snow and ice.

The four train Companies were stationed at VOLPAGE where they were subjected to a considerable amount of bombing which seemed to be a more general method of attack than on the Western Front.

1918.

On New Year's morning of 1918, the picquet on the horse lines of No. 2 Company was found in a pitiable state from a bomb dropped during the night, one man was dead when

1918.

the discovery was made, and the two others succumbed to their injuries immediately on being received in the hospital; a few of the horses were slightly wounded.

The Division moved into rest at RIESE, where the Train moved on January 19th. In February the Division again went into the Line at MONTEBELLUNA, but held its place only for a week when orders were received for a concentration in the CAMPOSAMPIERO area, preparatory to a return to France in view of the threatened German offensive on the Western Front.

Entraining began on March 2nd near MODANE. The train in which No. 3 Company was travelling broke its couplings on a descent, and the engine driver was for a time unaware of the accident. He then stopped his part of the train, into which the following part crashed with great force. Eight horses belonging to other Units were killed, two of the Train men were injured, two machine gunners were killed and four others injured.

No. 1 Company was left behind with the Artillery and followed a week later.

On March 5th the Train detrained at DOULLENS and MONDICOURT, and billetted in the LUCHEUX area.

A move was made to ACHIET-LE-PETIT on the 21st of March, staging one night on the way. On the night of

1918.

the 23rd, shelling of great severity took place all round the Camp, supplies were dumped by the M.T. in the Camp, and they were delivered forward on the 24th in the afternoon. The enemy shelled the Camp then, and wounded one man, blowing up two G.S. wagons loaded with supplies.

Orders to move Camp to MIRAMOUNT were received, and then altered to a field on the ACHIET-LE-PETIT - BOUCOY ROAD, where the train stood by till mid-night, when fresh orders came to move beyond BOUCOY. Owing to the immense amount of traffic on this road, it took five hours for the train to get out of the field in which it was standing. On arrival at this new point, orders came to retire still further this time to BIENVILLERS.

Before reaching this point, the 1st Line Transport withdrawing with the Division came up, and the supplies on the Train wagons were delivered to them.

At five o'clock on the afternoon of the 25th, orders were given to move to ST. AMAND where the Train refilled, next morning moving by a circuitous route to BAILLEUL VAL, and rations were delivered to Brigades at BERLES-AU-BOIS late in the evening, and at 2 a.m. next morning to the Artillery Wagon lines.

On the 27th the Divisional Artillery was attached to the 62nd Division, and No. 1 Company proceeded with them, the other Companies remained another day with Head

1918.

quarters at BAILLEUL VAL, on the 28th it went to SAULTY, from there it moved to AUTHIE on the 29th, reaching PAS on April 1st and then to HALLOY. On April 3rd and 4th, the Companies entrained at FREVENT and PETIT HOUVIN for the POPERINGHE area, the Companies moving to VLAMERTINGHE on the 7th and 8th, where drawing by horse transport was recommenced from that railhead.

During the whole period of the withdrawal, the motor transport of the supply column never failed to make contact with the Train, and the Division was never without its supplies.

With the exception of the two G.S. wagons and horses blown up in the Camp at ACHIET-LE-PETIT, no material was lost throughout the whole retirement.

C O M M A N D I N G   O F F I C E R S.

MAJOR RYAN   -   APRIL 5th 1915
MAJOR J.H.B. PEYTON.   -   APRIL 26th 1915
MAJOR McNALTY.   -   MAY 16th 1915
MAJOR G.T. WRIGHT.   -   MAY 27th 1915
MAJOR D.C.E. GROSE.   -   JUNE 15th 1915
LIEUT. COLONEL W.W. MOLONY.   -   OCTOBER 5th 1915
LIEUT. COLONEL T. DOWLING.   -   AUGUST 13th 1917

APPENDIX "B"

HONOURS AND AWARDS.

****

DISTINGUISHED SERVICE ORDER.

Lieut. Col. W.W. MOLONY.   -   June 4th 1917.
Major P.W. PROCKTER.   -   January 1st 1918.

MILITARY CROSS.

Captain & Adj. J.B.W. HEATER - January 3rd 1918.

MILITARY MEDAL.

T4/065205. Dr. MELLERSH, H.J. - September 21st 1917.
 T/35626. Dr. TAYLOR, G.E. - September 21st 1917.

MENTION IN DESPATCHES.

Lieut. Col. W.W. MOLONY. - May 29th 1917.
Captain D.D. GALBRAITH. - May 29th 1917.
Captain L.S. LADD. - May 29th 1917.
Lieut. Col. T. DOWLING. - December 24th 1917.
Major P.W. PROCKTER. - December 24th 1917.
Captain B.W. PARKER. - December 24th 1917.
T4/057476. C.S.M. RILEY, P.S. December 24th 1917.

EXTRACT FROM ROUTINE ORDERS, SECOND ARMY, MARCH 27th 1917.

The Army Commander wishes to express his appreciation of the gallant conduct of No. T2/13473, Dr. J. GRAY, No. 3 Coy. 41st Division Train, under the following circumstances :-

On the morning of the 17th March 1917, a team of horses drawing a G.S. Wagon had run away and was coming at a gallop towards the Divisional Coal Dump. There was a large amount of waiting traffic at the dump, and Dr. Gray, seeing the danger succeeded at great personal risk in stopping the runaways. This prompt action no doubt averted a serious accident.

EXTRACT FROM G.R.O. BY GENERAL SIR H.C.O. PLUMER, COMMANDING IN CHIEF THE BRITISH FORCES IN ITALY. G.H.Q. DECEMBER 27th 1917.

80. GALLANT CONDUCT. The G.O.C. Commanding in Chief wishes to record his appreciation of the gallant conduct of No. T/36851 Dr. H. COLLIER, 41st Divisional Train, in the following circumstances :-

On December 13th 1917, a pair of horses harnessed to a G.S. wagon bolted over rough ground unseating the driver. Dr. Collier siezed the horses as they went by and tried to pull them up, but was knocked down by the near horse, and both the near wheels of the wagon passed over him. He had, however, sufficiently checked the pair to bring them to a standstill a short distance away.

APPENDIX "C"

CASUALTIES AMONGST PERSONNEL.

KILLED.

2/Lieut. G. WARRINGTON.	- August 18th 1917.
T2/11241 Corporal HASTINGS, D.	- May 28th 1917.
T4/233814 Dr. WIGGINS, G.W.	- August 4th 1917.
T3/026871 Dr. LAIRD, W.	- January 1st 1918.
T4/094206 Dr. CROCKER, S.J.	- April 17th 1918.

WOUNDED.

Lieut. W.S. MAILE.	- April 30th 1917.
2/Lieut. S. COOKSON.	- August 18th 1917.
T4/062033 Dr. COX, J.	- January 6th 1917.
T3/026587 Dr. STEVENS, J.G.	- January 6th 1917.
T/36548 Dr. MINSLULL, J.	- May 28th 1917.
T1/4373 Dr. CULLEN, P.	- July 27th 1917.
T3/027002 Sgt. HAMILTON, A.	- August 7th 1918.
S4/043970 S.Sgt. KEEFE, W.	- April 17th 1918.
T3/027003 Dr. MURRAY, M.	- April 17th 1918.
S4/042242 Cpl. BARON, W.	- April 17th 1918.
T/37205 Dr. MITTEN, J.	- April 17th 1918.

GASSED.

T2/SR.03774 Dr. STEEL, C.J.	- June 1st 1917.
T/28228 Dr. GRANT, W.E.	- June 1st 1917.
T4/057437 Dr. CHURCHILL, W.A.M.	- June 4th 1917.

APPENDIX "D"

CASUALTIES TO HORSES AND VEHICLES.

✶✶✶✶✶✶✶✶✶✶✶✶✶✶✶✶✶✶✶✶✶✶✶✶✶✶✶✶✶✶✶✶✶

HORSES.

KILLED. 34

WOUNDED. 36

VEHICLES.

TOTALLY DESTROYED. 14

EVACUATED. 3

REPAIRED IN THE FIELD. 11

JB   APPENDIX "E"

COMPANY MOVES.
****

| DATE. | PLACE AT WHICH UNIT HAS SERVED. |

1915.

MARCH.	ALDERSHOT.
1st APRIL.	FRENSHAM PLACE.
25th SEPTEMBER.	MILFORD CAMP.
8th NOVEMBER.	MYTCHETT CAMP.
14th NOVEMBER.	PANGBOURNE.

1916.

FEBRUARY.	MYTCHETT.
2nd MAY.	SOUTHAMPTON.
2nd MAY.	HAVRE.
3rd MAY.	STEENBECQUE.
4th MAY.	STRAZEELE.
30th MAY.	LA CRECHE.
17th AUGUST.	FLETRE.
24th AUGUST.	LONG.
5th SEPTEMBER.	ARGOLUVES.
7th SEPTEMBER.	BUIRE.
11th SEPTEMBER.	ALBERT.
18th SEPTEMBER.	BUIRE.
2nd OCTOBER.	BECORDEL.
4th OCTOBER.	QUARRY.
11th OCTOBER.	BUIRE.
16th OCTOBER.	ARGOLUVES.
18th OCTOBER.	HALLANCOURT.
20th OCTOBER.	FLETRE.
24th OCTOBER.	RENINGHELST.

1917.

1st JULY.	METEREN.
23rd JULY.	BOESCHEPE.
26th JULY.	WESTOUTRE.
15th AUGUST.	METERAN.
21st AUGUST.	WIZERNES.
15th SEPTEMBER.	ZERECOTEN.
23rd SEPTEMBER.	CAESTRE.
27th SEPTEMBER.	LA PANNE.
7th OCTOBER.	ST. IDESBALDE.
29th OCTOBER.	ROSENDAEL.
11th NOVEMBER.	LOON PLAGE.
17th NOVEMBER.	CANNETO. (ITALY).
17th NOVEMBER.	ACQUANEGRA.
19th NOVEMBER.	GOITO.
20th NOVEMBER.	IREVENZUOLO.
22nd NOVEMBER.	OPPEANO.
23rd NOVEMBER.	ST. STEFANO.
24th NOVEMBER.	ALBETTENO.
25th NOVEMBER.	VILLA KERIAN.
26th NOVEMBER.	VILLA DEL CONTE.
28th NOVEMBER.	LEVADA.
2nd DECEMBER.	SELVA.

APPENDIX "E"

COMPANY MOVES. (Contd).

DATE.	PLACE AT WHICH UNIT HAS SERVED.
1918.	
19th JANUARY.	RIESE.
18th FEBRUARY.	MONTEBELLUNA.
26th FEBRUARY.	COMPOSAMPIERO.
6th MARCH.	DOULLENS. (France).
6th MARCH.	LUCHEUX.
21st MARCH.	BRESLE.
22nd MARCH.	ACHIET-LE-PETIT.
25th MARCH.	BIENVILLER DU BOIS.
25th MARCH.	ST AMAND.
26th MARCH.	BAILLEUVAL.
28th MARCH.	GOMBREMETZ.
29th MARCH.	AUTHIE.
2nd APRIL.	PAS.
3rd APRIL.	HALLOY.
4th APRIL.	STEENVOORDE.
10th APRIL.	BRANDHOCK

JB.   APPENDIX "F"

PRIZES WON AT HORSE SHOWS.

****

DIVISIONAL HORSE SHOW.

SEPTEMBER 1916.   1st PRIZE. 1 Pair H.D. & LIMBER.
               Tie for 1st PRIZE. 1 Pair MULES & LIMBER.

JUNE 1917.   1st PRIZE. 1 Pair L.D. & G.S. WAGON.
                  1st PRIZE. 1 Pair H.D. & G.S. WAGON.
                  1st PRIZE. N.C.O.s Jumping Competition.

JULY 1917.   1st PRIZE. 1 Pair H.D. & G.S. WAGON.
                  2nd PRIZE   1 Pair MULES & LIMBER.

FEBRUARY 1918.   1st PRIZE. 1 Pair H.D. & G.S. WAGON.
                  2nd PRIZE. 1 Pair H.D. & G.S. WAGON.

BRIGADE HORSE SHOW.

123rd I. BRigade, 124th I. Brigade May 1917.

        1st PRIZE. 1 H.D. shewn in bridle.
        1st PRIZE. Watercart and turnout complete
        1st PRIZE. Officers Charger.
        2nd PRIZE. Officers Charger.
        2nd PRIZE. 1 Pair H.D. & G.S. Wagon.

www.ingramcontent.com/pod-product-compliance
Lightning Source LLC
Chambersburg PA
CBHW081353160426
43192CB00013B/2400